The Minister and the Funeral

The Minister and the Funeral

A Pastor's Primer on the Funeral

Including Sermons and Illustrations

By
Frank R. Shivers

LIGHTNING SOURCE
1246 Heil Quaker Blvd.
La Vergne, TN

Unless otherwise noted, Scripture quotations are
from
The Holy Bible *King James Version*

Library of Congress Cataloging-in-Publication Data

Shivers, Frank R., 1949-
Spurs to Soul Winning / Frank Shivers
ISBN 978-1-878127-19-8

Library of Congress Control Number:
2013910929

Cover design by
Tim King of Click Graphics, Inc.

For Information:
Frank Shivers Evangelistic Association
P. O. Box 9991
Columbia, South Carolina 29290
www.frankshivers.com

Presented to

_____

By_____

Date_____

Our church members quickly forget our sermons, but they remember our kindnesses, especially those dark hours when we were walking with them in the valley.[1]

—Warren Wiersbe

The clouds may at times veil my sky. Sorrows and difficulties may try my soul. New discoveries of the corruption of my own heart may bring humiliation and repentance. But this peace with God remains unchanged, for it rests not on me, not on my frames of mind or experiences, but on the finished work of Christ and the testimony of the Word of God, of which it is written: "For ever, O LORD, thy word is settled in heaven."[2]

—H. A. Ironside

To

Dr. Jim Palmer

A pastor with the evangelist's heart whose prompting led to the writing of this book. Thank you, Jim, for fueling my flame to write and the continuous encouragement given in my ministry as a vocational evangelist.

"The Lord GOD has put his Spirit in me,
because the LORD has appointed me to tell
the good news to the poor.
He has sent me to comfort those whose
hearts are broken,
to tell the captives they are free,
and to tell the prisoners they are released."
(Isaiah 61:1 NCV)

Contents

Preface

I was encouraged by a senior pastor of many years to write and make available to both the young and new pastor a primer on the funeral. The present volume is in response to that request.

Andrew W. Blackwood, the great preaching professor, said there are two kinds of ministers: the kind who knows how to conduct a funeral, and the other who does not.[3] At times, even for those who know the how, funerals can be staggering; for none are exactly alike, because no two people grieve the same. Caring for and comforting people in the hour of grave sorrow doubtlessly is one of the greatest challenges and privileges afforded to the man of God.[4]

Senior pastors certainly agree with Warren Wiersbe's assessment regarding the funeral: "No pastoral responsibility is more demanding than ministering comfort to people who are shocked and bereaved because of the death of a loved one."[5] This primer on the funeral is purposed to help the pastor meet this responsibility preparedly and effectively, without fear or anxiety, and with greater ease in fulfilling God's call echoed by Isaiah, "Comfort ye, comfort ye my people, saith your God" (Isaiah 40:1).

1

Funeral Sermon

The most difficult part of the ministry is ministering to a person whose loved one just passed away.[6]

—John Bisagno

At a wedding, I may feel like a necessary accessory along with the flowers, rented tuxedos, and candles; but at a funeral, I sense people sincerely look to me for help. People are more open and responsive, appreciative of help given—more than at any other time.[7]

—Calvin Ratz

A prevailing fault of funeral discourses is the occupation of too much time with generalities or truths that have no special application to the existing circumstances. It is far better to confine such discourses to narrower limits and to that particular range of thought which all will recognize to be pertinent.[8]

—J. A. Broadus, Professor of Preaching

I am, however, so averse to the preaching of what are called funeral sermons that I forbear, lest I appear to eulogize the creature when my only aim should be to magnify the grace of God.[9]

—C. H. Spurgeon

A Sympathizing Shepherd

"It doesn't really matter whether you grip the arms of the dentist's chair or let your hands lie in your lap. The drill drills on."[10]

—C. S. Lewis reference to mourning

Prior to the funeral sermon, the pastor must be a sympathizing shepherd to the deceased family. To love on the grieving and to cry with them will comfort and encourage more than any words that may be spoken.

A little girl told her mother that a classmate at school was very sad. Upon the mother's inquiry as to why, the girl replied, "Because her mother has died."

"And what did you do to help the little girl?" the mother asked.

The child answered, "I just sat down by her side at the desk and cried, too."[11]

The caring ministry of "weep with them that weep" (Romans 12:15) cannot be overstated. Job's friends sat and wept with him for seven days without saying a word (Job 2:12–13).

What to Say

"Caregivers wonder," declares Wayne Oates, *"What shall I say? What can I do?* Yet these questions are secondary to our being a presence, a reminder of the presence of God in Jesus Christ, that the sufferers are not alone. We are sharers with them of their burdens as we fulfill the law of Christ (Galatians 6:2). Our own self-awareness of this being with them prompts us to give thanks that neither they nor we are alone; the Presence of God is with us, bearing the pain, agony, and desolation with us. Jesus told us He would not leave us desolate, literally "as orphans" (John 14:18), in times of crises when severe tragedy strikes. Thus it is not what we can say or do; it is what we are, who we can be, the kind of presence we bring to them, whom we represent—the Lord Jesus Christ."[12]

What to Avoid Saying

"In their grief people may ask, 'Why, God?'" declares Paul Powell. 'Why did this happen to me?' Don't be a glib Bible quoter. Simplistic answers to complex questions are not only unhelpful; they can be harmful. Statements like, 'This is God's will,' or 'God knows best,' are theologically shallow and provide little or no comfort. It is better to hear their questions as cries of pain rather than literal questions."[13]

Refrain from statements like "I know how you feel" (you really don't); "It will take time, but you will get through this" (though true, it gives nothing for them to cling to now); "Everything will be okay" (but it's not okay; their heart is in a crucible of tremendous pain); "Everything works together for good" (truth for sure, but to someone whose eyes are blinded with tears of tremendous grief, perhaps not very comforting—at least presently). In the initial visit to the home, it's not the words said but your presence that ministers most.

The first meeting with the family is not the time to discuss funeral arrangements, except for whom they desire to have conduct the service. Heartache and grief are softened by the fragrance of the pastor's presence, so after speaking to the family, simply linger awhile. Prior to departure, read choice Scripture texts that will comfort, and pray with the family.

Purpose of the Funeral Sermon

The funeral service is the most trying duty of the pastor. To the sorrowing friends there is no loss so great as their loss. If the pastor's address does not appreciate this, and if he does not pour oil into the wounds, he has failed them at the most critical time.[14]

—F. M. Barton

The one thing that warrants such a relationship as subsists between you and me [his congregation at Manchester] is this—my consciousness that I have a message from God and your belief that you hear such from my lips.[15]

—Alexander Maclaren

The purpose of the funeral sermon is fourfold.

Infuse Comfort

"Whenever you preach at a funeral," said a Southern gentlewoman to the pastor of a neighboring church, "you always try to bring the comfort of God."

The minister expressed his thanks and then asked, "Pardon me, but what else could I attempt to do?"

"I scarcely know," was the reply, "but you are the only clergyman in town who always uses the funeral service as a means of bringing Christian comfort."[16]

What a reputation to earn as a minister! The funeral sermon is to be Gospel-centered, built with the choicest biblical lumber of soul comfort under the leadership of the Holy Spirit delivered with utter compassion. Its primary purpose is to render comfort and hope to the bereaved by the declaration of what God says about the death of a saint and the message of the resurrection of Jesus Christ. "Wherefore comfort one another with these words" (I Thessalonians 4:18).

> There is a balm in Gilead
> To make the wounded whole.
> There is a balm in Gilead
> To heal the sin-sick soul.
>   —African-American Spiritual

Instill Hope

When you are ministering in funerals, the believers and unbelievers alike remember the sermon is not for the one in the casket but for those in the pew. "The preeminence of Christ our Redeemer," states Harry L. Reeder, "and the truth of the Gospel with the glorious promise of the resurrection must be simply, thoughtfully, and clearly articulated. Your challenge is that everyone in attendance has to undergo a paradigm shift. Most of your listeners believe their loved one or friend has just gone from 'the land of the living' to 'the land of the dying.' You must proclaim to them that the exact opposite is actually true. They have not left the 'land of the living' to go to the 'land of the dying'; they have left the 'land of the dying' to go to 'the land of the living.'[17]

Death does not have the final say-so about our bodies. Jesus does, and He says, "I am the resurrection, and the life: he that believeth in me, though he were dead, yet shall he live" (John 11:25). This is the believer's hope in Christ Jesus.

Not only is the sermon purposed to give hope to the saved but to proclaim to the unsaved that man's only hope temporally and eternally is in a personal relationship with Jesus Christ.

Initiate Healing

In summarizing Granger E. Westberg on a key essential of the funeral sermon cited in *Good Grief*, author Perry Biddle, Jr., states: "One of the most helpful things about the funeral message is that it may address the mourning process the bereaved are just beginning. The sermon should deal honestly with the reality of death, pointing out that the grief wound cannot heal fully until one has accepted the reality of the loss."[18]

Impart Honor

To pay tribute to the life of the deceased ones for their contribution to their family, church, community, and the Kingdom of God is appropriate and is healing medicine to the grief wound of family and friends.

The Funeral Sermon

More than other sermons, the funeral sermon demands brevity while encompassing much. In the pastor's fifteen to twenty minutes, he must sum up the life of the deceased and pay tribute to it, render comfort and hope from God's Word to the family and friends, and passionately compel the lost to trust Christ, all without the appearance of being hurried. To succeed in this paramount task requires serious preparation undergirded with earnest prayer. Grief expert Harold Ivan Smith has said, "The historic advice, 'take it to the Lord in prayer,' is wise for grievers and pastors alike. From the first moments of notification, the pastor-leader is praying, 'Lord, guide me.'"[19]

Unlike other sermons, the funeral sermon has to be prepared expeditiously due to the brevity of time between notification of a death and the funeral. To be somewhat ready for this hasty undertaking, maintain a sermon seed file specifically for funerals and study rich texts on which to build such a sermon on a regular basis, making notes as you proceed. With such discipline, the pastor will never be without immediate help in jumpstarting the funeral message.

Personalize the Sermon

A funeral director shared that at times family members tell him following the funeral service not enough was said about their loved one. "The preacher didn't do right by him/her," and they left disappointed. Obviously in services where this is the case, the pastor does not have next Sunday to make it right. Sadly, he blew his one chance. Such a danger couches at the door of every funeral the minister conducts. So how can the minister "do right" by the deceased while at the same time faithfully proclaiming the Gospel?

Inquire of family members what they wish incorporated into the funeral service. Lovingly ask regarding the deceased, "How would you best describe his/her life?" "Was he/she a Christian; and, if so, was he/she active in the church?" "What was his/her favorite Bible text/hymn?" "Using adjectives, how might you describe his/her life?" "What memories of your loved one do you endear above others?"

It may be helpful to scan through the Bible of the deceased to ascertain such information (some pastors like to preach the funeral from the Bible belonging to the deceased one and give it to the closest family member at the conclusion). In ministering to people on their death-beds, the pastor may lovingly, tactfully acquire memories, stories, experiences, and other facts to share in the funeral sermon. I recall ministering to Andy, a teenager with cancer, for nearly a year, during which time I was able to lead him to faith in Christ and prepare him for death. In my last visit with him, I asked what he would like for me to share in his funeral. Telling family/friends that Andy asked me to share not only the fact of his salvation but the very means of it was forceful.

Be Truthful

Truth is an essential in preaching the funeral sermon. "No promptings of his own sorrow," states John Broadus, "or regard for the feelings of others must lead him [the pastor] to the exaggerated praises which are so natural."[20]

A (hopefully) fictitious story is told of a lady who, when hearing the preacher speak of the nice things about her husband at his funeral, finally got up, walked to the casket, and looked inside to make sure she was in the right place. Don't present the deceased as better or greater people than they were or give inference that they went to Heaven despite never having made a profession of faith in Jesus Christ. Such is not only a travesty but an injury to the Gospel, distorting biblical truth.

Robert Hughes cautions, "The preacher is certainly to personalize the sermon, but without lauding the dead."[21] John A. Broadus counsels, "In general, the preacher ought to exercise reserve in what he says of the departed; and in the case of wicked people, it is frequently in the best taste and shows the most real kindness to say nothing."[22] Paul W. Powell emphasizes Broadus' statement in advising, "Don't talk too much about the deceased. Focus mostly on Jesus Christ."[23]

The Hinge Is Jesus Christ

Despite the need to share somewhat of the deceased one's story, *His Story* must be paramount in the sermon. I concur with Robert Hughes who said, "The most effective text for funeral sermons is a hinge. At the grave of Lazarus we not only see Jesus weep, but we hear the good news, 'I am the resurrection and the life' (John 11:25). In the upper room we not only sense the disciples' fear, but we hear the reassuring, 'Peace be with you' (John 20:19). In the midst of these narratives the action shifts from human anguish to God's promise of help."[24] But what is the hinge that should be interwoven throughout the funeral sermon? It is that of the death, burial and resurrection of Jesus Christ and what that means to the deceased and their family and friends seated before you. W. A. Criswell counsels that the pastor should speak about the fundamental, basic verities of life, death, earth, Heaven, time, and eternity. Further, Criswell cautions, "To waste the hour in drivel with cheap eulogy and empty ostentation is to sin against the presence of the Holy Spirit. Speak the message of God. They will hear it as never before when they are seated in the service before you."[25]

Don't Shoehorn a Text

In preparing the funeral sermon, don't just jump into the Bible with the attempt to "shoehorn" a text, making it applicable to comfort, hope or encouragement; rather, allow such to flow naturally from a text. As with any sermon text, that of the funeral is determined by prayer, dissected by study (exegesis), developed by its objective, and delivered with power. Alexander Gregg surmises that "there are three things to aim at in public speaking [and I add funeral preaching]: first, to get into your subject; then, to get your subject into yourself; and, lastly, to get your subject into your hearers."[26]

Keep It Brief

The sermon should be relatively simple and short (no longer than 15 to 20 minutes) compassionately delivered. C. H. Spurgeon advises the preacher to spend more time in the study, so to spend less in the pulpit.[27] That council is never more expedient to heed than in the funeral sermon.

Avoid "Preaching Someone into Heaven or Hell"

In funeral messages for strangers (spiritual state an unknown), don't make a presumption about their eternal estate. Instead, in it and in the funeral of an unbeliever [Unknown to the minister, the person may have had a "death-bed conversion" as the thief on the cross.] allow the Gospel presentation to make that revelation. Using this approach, you will never be guilty of attempting to preach someone into Heaven or into Hell, which sadly occurs far more often than supposed. In *On the Preparation and Delivery of Sermons,* John A. Broadus declares, "When the departed was not a Christian, he [the pastor] may sometimes lawfully speak a few soothing words as to anything which specially endeared the deceased to his friends. But this must be done, if done at all, without exaggeration; and it is a solemn duty to avoid saying one word which suggests that these good points of character afford any ground of hope for eternity....Nay, if the deceased did not give evidence of being regenerate, a believer in Christ, let us say nothing about his eternal future—nothing whatever."[28]

Haddon Robinson concurs with Blackwood: "It is completely inappropriate to suggest that the deceased has gone to a place of eternal damnation." Robinson continues, "That might be a true statement, but the preacher is not God and cannot know the heart of the person. Much better is the approach that all of us are mortal and need to deal with the question of eternity."[29]

Preview What Others Will Read or Sing

Regarding the reading of poetry or other literature and special music in the funeral service by family or friends, the pastor must ascertain its theological suitability (Does it violate Scripture?) and applicability. Save the family and yourself possible grief and embarrassment by requesting all who participate in the service to notify you up-front of their musical or literary selection.

The Funeral Sermon Structure

Text

C. H. Spurgeon, when asked how to select a text, told his students, "Cry to God for it."[30] Andrew W. Blackwood said the funeral text should, as a rule, be short, clear and luminous; not need much interpretation; arrest attention; and fasten to the memory.[31]

The Proposition Sentence

The proposition sentence is a concise sentence that states the essence of the sermon. It is the "hub" from which the spokes (preaching points) develop. The proposition is the gist of the sermon, the sermon condensed into one sentence, the spinal column running through the message. Fred Craddock states, "No preacher has the right to look for points until he has the point."[32]

The Objective Sentence

The objective sentence concisely states the purpose of the sermon, that which you hope to accomplish in its delivery.

The Transitional Sentence

The introduction transitional sentence is like a hitch on a train engine that hooks it to the cars it is to pull. It is the major connector from introduction to the body of the sermon. The transition sentences within the body of the sermon hook main point to main point and then to the invitation.

The Body of the Sermon or Outline

The body of the sermon contains an introduction, two or more points, illustrations, and invitation (conclusion) all built around the funeral text selected.

Introduction

I prefer short introductions encapsulating the substance and purpose of the sermon. Don't keep the grieving family/friends on the front porch too long (introduction); invite them into the house (body of sermon). I have found helpful in setting the tone for the funeral service the words of the Doxology. Upon rising to speak I share,

> Praise God, from Whom all blessings flow;
> Praise Him, all creatures here below;
> Praise Him above, ye heavenly host;
> Praise Father, Son, and Holy Ghost.

Next, I say, "We have gathered here today to glorify God and honor the life and home going of _____." (If the deceased was a believer)

The body of the sermon flows from the analysis of the text. The preaching points should flow easily one to the other, building upon the "preaching point" of the sermon and progressing toward the invitational appeal. The outline of the sermon should be easy to follow. The length of the sermon, as previously stated, should be confined to 15 to 20 minutes, with the total service being no more than 45 minutes.

Illustrations

C. H. Spurgeon said, "The sermon is the house; the illustrations are the windows that let in the light."[33] H. A. Ironside commented regarding the place of illustrations in the sermon, "Most minds are so constituted that they need illustrations to enable them readily to grasp the full import of the message. Our Lord Himself used this method continually; and in this, as in other things, He has left 'us an example, that ye should follow his steps.'"[34]

Bridge to the Invitation

The transitional sentence to the invitation from the preaching points bridges the sermon to the decision desired. It is helpful either to memorize the sentence or have it clearly written for recall at this point in the sermon delivery.

For a more in-depth study of the construction and delivery of a sermon, see my book *Evangelistic Preaching 101.*

Types of Funeral Sermons

With the funeral sermon there are four primary approaches.

Expository Approach.

"At its best, expository preaching," states Haddon Robinson "is the presentation of biblical truth, derived from and transmitted through a historical, grammatical, Spirit-guided study of a passage in its context, which the Holy Spirit applies first to the life of the preacher and then through him to his congregation."[35] John Stott emphasizes that "The expository preacher is a bridge builder, seeking to span the gulf between the Word of God and the mind of man. He must do his utmost to interpret the Scriptures so accurately and plainly and to apply them so forcefully that the truth crosses the bridge."[36]

Textual Approach.

"The main lines of development are drawn from the text itself, and the main outline is kept strictly within the limits of the text."[37] It has been called the expository sermon in miniature.

Topical Approach.

The minister chooses a topic for the sermon and selects Scripture to support it. The sermon stands independently of a biblical text.

Expositional Eulogy Approach.

Expositional eulogies are like any expository sermon, states Dr. Jerry Barlow, Professor of preaching at New Orleans Baptist Theological Seminary. "Based on an appropriate biblical text, an expositional eulogy is an expository homiletical discourse, but one characterized in content and method by this intentional difference: the life of the deceased person is used as 'light' throughout the development of the funeral exposition. In essence, an expositional eulogy is an expository homiletical discourse which can present both tribute and testimony in celebrating the deceased person's life and, more importantly for deceased Christians, give a comforting and compelling witness in lifting up Christ and applicable biblical truths. While traditional eulogies may be 'generally considered out of order in Christian worship...because they do not bring glory to God,' expositional eulogies certainly can, in fulfillment of Matt. 5:14, 16."[38]

Be Biblical

"Whether or not we expound the Bible topically or textually," states Stephen Olford, "we still need to exegete the Scriptures if we are going to validate what we are going to say as God's truth. We must ever remember those famous words of Augustine, 'When the Scriptures speak, God speaks.'"[39]

Referring to preaching in general (therefore applicable to the funeral sermon), Karl Bath writes,

"Preaching must be exposition of Holy Scripture. I have not to talk *about* Scripture but *from* it."[40]

The Evangelistic Appeal

If these sheep who are outside the fold find no spiritual power, no vision of the eternal realities of life, no abiding consciousness of the living Christ [in the sermon], then they shall be content to remain outside.[41]

—Earl Daniels

Funeral services prompt the unsaved to think about death and eternity, which is a rarity for most unbelievers, so don't shortchange this part of the sermon. Unlike the case in a church service, in the funeral one's defenses are lowered due to various grief factors, creating a good climate of receptivity of the Gospel. "It has been the experience of clergy," states Robert Hughes, "that greater vulnerability leads to heightened receptivity more often than to stubborn defensiveness."[42] Tactfully but pungently make clear that entrance into Heaven is only possible through Jesus Christ. The invitation need not be public (walking the aisle) but can be issued in saying, "Now, right where you are seated, you may enter into a personal relationship with Jesus Christ by inviting Him into your heart. I will lead you in that prayer." You may say, "John (name of the deceased) became a Christian many years ago and would want me to invite you to make that same decision so that life may be lived to its fullest and Heaven one day become your eternal home."

Encourage all who make such decisions in private to share it with you in the aftermath of the service. Evangelistic tracts that simply point the way of salvation and its urgency may be distributed to each in attendance prior to or after the funeral service.

The Sermon Delivery

Utilize the tone/volume of voice in preaching the sermon that will convey both God's and your caring compassion. It's not the loud, harsh, screaming-sounding voice that will connect with the broken hearted, but rather the gentle, warm, natural voice. Avoid incomprehensible words and doctrinal treatises in the effort to comfort the family and reach the unreached. Look the grieving family and friends in the eye, making connection with their hearts as you speak. Preach *to* them, not *at* them. Additionally, in preaching funeral sermons, curtail pacing the floor, remaining more stationary. The act of preaching a funeral is far different from preaching on Sunday morning or in a revival meeting, for it is a different kind of ministry. As such, it calls for a different style in delivery than that to which you have perhaps been accustomed. Include the message of salvation and an invitation to respond to Jesus Christ as Lord and Savior.

The Sermon's Power

The secret of the minister's power in ministering to the bereaved is revealed by Isaiah. "The Spirit of the Lord GOD is upon me; because the LORD hath anointed me to preach good tidings unto the meek; he hath sent me to bind up the brokenhearted, to proclaim liberty to the captives, and the opening of the prison to them that are bound" (Isaiah 61:1).

Commenting on the text, the great London pastor C. H. Spurgeon wrote, "The one who speaks for God should speak in God's strength because the Spirit of God has come upon him, is moving him to speak, is helping him while speaking, and will make the word which he proclaims to be quick and powerful. To attempt to preach in any other power is to ensure failure."[43] Spurgeon continues, "There can be no broken hearts mended or captives set free where the Spirit of God is not honored."[44] To heal the broken hearts of those who are being ministered to, it is imperative that the power of God rests upon you. Otherwise your words will merely be 'tinkling cymbals and sounding brass' without avail.

The Family /Friend Eulogy

A *eulogy* is defined as "a laudatory speech or written tribute, especially one praising someone who has died."[45] Its synonyms include *tribute, commendation,* and *accolade.* Due to the common misuse of the eulogy by ministers over the years, its very mention rings with disapproval and avoidance. However, the eulogy, if properly issued, may prove acceptable and beneficial. Perhaps if we exchanged the word *tribute* for *eulogy* it would be better received and more understandable: "We have come to pay tribute to the life and works of John Doe."

John R. Bisagno stated, "On occasion there will be a eulogy or testimony by a family member or friend about the deceased. It is important that these be few and brief. A ten-minute eulogy is seven or eight minutes too long. If eulogies are given at all, there should be no more than two, one by a family member and one by a friend."[46]

A benefit of the eulogy is that it provides healing therapy to the person who delivers it and perhaps to others as well. Its danger lies in that the minister loses control of what is declared, opening the door for biblical heresy or just plain untruth.

W. A. Criswell, legendary pastor of the First Baptist Church, Dallas, Texas, for over fifty years worked around that potential. By phone, he would request that the most immediate member of the family of the deceased write out a page or two about the person. He in turn would read the eulogy at the funeral, citing that the family had written it.[47] In doing this, Criswell kept each funeral service unique, personal, and under his control with regard to time and proclamation. You as I have no doubt witnessed a funeral that for the most part was comprised of nothing but eulogies. Such services that take family members down memory lane, though beneficial, fall short of providing the comfort and hope the family needs, which comes only from God's Word delivered by God's man. The minister's primary task is to preach to the living, not eulogize the dead! If family members request to share a eulogy, ask them to write it out. This will prevent rambling, guard the time, and help them should they be overcome with emotion.[48]

A Dead Funeral

Burne Jones attended the funeral for Robert Browning, the famous British poet, and became distraught at the coldness it entailed. He knew Browning well enough to know his life was one of joy and hope, neither of which the funeral service reflected. Browning's optimistic view of life and death is reflected in the following poem he authored.

Grow old along with me!
The best is yet to be,
The last of life, for which the first was made.
Our times are in His hand,
Who saith, "A whole I planned;
Youth shows but half. Trust God, see all, nor be afraid!"[49]

Jones became so deeply disturbed over what he felt and heard in the service that he wrote, "As I sat there and listened to that dead funeral service, I thought of the intensive life of Robert Browning, who all of his days down to his old age was alive and young in his heart and spirit. I just wished someone would come out of the triforium [a gallery forming an upper story to the aisle of a church and typically an arcaded story between the nave arches and clerestory][50] with a trumpet and blast the sound, raise the dead, wake the people, and speak of victory and resurrection."[51] The pastor must ever guard against conducting a "dead funeral."

Don't Muddle

The caring ministry of the pastor to the family and the sermon he delivers potentially have the power to console, to encourage, to evangelize, to develop/restore relationships, to reclaim the church dropout for active Christian service, and to edify believers all to the glory of God. To ignore such an opportunity is foolish; to fail to redeem such an opportunity by neglect of doing due diligence in sermon preparation and/or rendering comfort to the family is deplorable. For sure, you have many pressing demands of ministry, but such are not an excuse to muddle through the sermon or ministry to the family. As Andrew W. Blackwood stated, "Death comes but once; there should be no ministerial muddling. Our God is no muddler."[52]

Keep Records

In the aftermath of the funeral, affix to the sermon the name of the deceased for whom the sermon was preached and the date it was delivered.

The Ten Commandments for Funeral Messages

I

THOU SHALT NOT BEAR FALSE WITNESS. Tell the truth—not necessarily the whole truth, but nothing but the truth. You can do yourself and the church a lot of harm by bearing false witness. If you depart from the truth in a funeral sermon, the community will rightly suspect that you are likely to do the same at other times.

II

THOU SHALT REMEMBER THAT SYMPATHY WILL COVER A MULTITUDE OF HOMILETICAL SINS. There is no substitute for it. If people feel that you really care for them and that you feel the burden of their sorrow, they will overlook a lot of mistakes. But if they suspect that you are simply talking shop, merely expressing words of consolation which you do not feel, then your ministry to their bereavement is doomed to failure.

III

THOU SHALT NOT BE HEARD FOR THY MUCH SPEAKING. The value of your words to the bereaved family is not to be measured by the length of your sermon. After the first fifteen or twenty minutes, they will probably hear little that you say. A short, simple message is more fitting than long-winded oratory.

IV

THOU SHALT BEWARE OF DEATHBED STORIES. A funeral service is difficult enough for the bereaved family without the unnecessary punishment of such phrases as "this grim monster of death" and heartrending repetition of pathetic last moments.

V

THOU SHALT FIT THE MESSAGE TO THE OCCASION. The same suit will not fit every man. Neither will the same funeral message fit every occasion. Let there be such individuality about the sermon as there is in made-to-measure clothes.

VI

THOU SHALT NOT CRY WITH A LOUD VOICE. There are perhaps times and occasions for such speaking, but not at a funeral service.

VII

THOU SHALT NOT PROCLAIM THY DOUBTS. Those who are present at the funeral service have their full share of burdens without your adding to them. What is there in your religious belief to meet the desolate hour of death? If you have some strong, clear word of assurance that will bring out the rainbow of hope in the midst of the clouds of doubts, you may be sure of an attentive audience. What they desire is not questions raised, but questions answered.

VIII

THOU SHALT NOT DENOUNCE. Far better is that wooing note which comes out of a sincere sorrow for the tragedy that has befallen the deceased.

IX

THOU SHALT NOT HARP UPON ONE STRING. There are many beautiful themes in the symphony of faith. Let us not be mere dispensers of patent medicine, a cure-all for every ill; let us rather as a discriminating physician adapt our treatment to the need of the patient.

X

THOU SHALT REMEMBER ALWAYS THY AMBASSA-DORSHIP. You are Christ's representative. Standing in the presence of death, you speak for the Lord of Life. By your presentation of the Gospel, your Christ will be judged.[53]

2
Difficult Funerals

We trust our Sovereign God because He has shown us His heart at the cross. There, where any one of us would have stood and cried out, "This is wrong; God you must stop this," our Savior made Heaven's good come out of earth's worst tragedy. At the cross we learn that God is good and can be trusted, even when everything seems wrong to human sight.[54]

—Bryan Chappell

Preaching difficult funerals (sudden death, suicide, murder, accident, and the death of children—not that all are not somewhat difficult) is challenging due to their nature and the time restraint both in preparation and presentation. The following guidelines for difficult funerals hopefully will be of help when you are faced with such an assignment.

Be Compassionate

"Mourn with those that mourn," regardless of the nature of their loved one's death, lifestyle, or beliefs.

Come Across That It's Not "Business As Usual"

Don't give the perception you are there because it's your "job." It will be overly obvious if it's business as usual for the minister rather than heartfelt ministry.

Mention the Cause of Death

Address the cause of death (with the family's approval) with tactful compassion. "Mentioning the cause of death gives everyone present the chance to start recovering from grief from a more-or-less common starting point."[55]

Answer What You Can

Anxious hearts are waiting for answers to questions that may bring hope and comfort, therefore answer if you possibly can. Theological answers (not speculations) simply stated can greatly enhance grief recovery and relieve the bereaved from personal answer searching in the Bible.

Upon the mind of family/friends at the funeral of one who took his own life are searching questions. Wilson Benton in the sermon "Suicide of a Christian Leader" suggests several questions that ought be answered in such a funeral sermon: Is suicide the unpardonable sin?, Do Christians commit suicide?, What is the eternal state of one who takes his own life?, Are others to blame for the suicide?, Do God's promises still apply to the person who commits suicide?, and What shall we do?[56] Clarifying that suicide does not nullify salvation (God's promises still apply) and that family members are not to blame for their loved one's act promotes mental and spiritual healing.

With regard to a child's death, different questions arise that are answerable: Where was God when my child died?, Where is my child?, Will I ever see my child again?, Is my child lonely for me?, What is my child doing in Heaven?, What is the good that God designs to have occur from my child's death?, How can I live without my child? In answering the question with regard to babies being in Heaven, Dr. Ron Herrod declares, "The answer is yes and no. *All babies go to Heaven*—they are not saved but are safe in the hands of Jesus. David said regarding the death of his child, 'The child cannot come to me but I can go to the child' (2 Samuel 12:23). *But there are no helpless people in Heaven*. Upon the death of Christian invalids in nursing homes and elsewhere they are carried by the angels into Heaven where there is no more pain, no more sorrow, and no more death. And they are no longer invalid. Just as there are no invalids in Heaven, there are no helpless infants. My late friend Angel Martinez used to say, 'We will all be 33 years old forever in Heaven.' He based that belief on Scripture which states that we will be like Jesus in Heaven (1 John 3:2; Philippians 3:21), and He was approximately 33 when He ascended back to Heaven."[57]

"When parents experience the death of a child [like David in Scripture]," remarks John MacArthur, "one of the first questions they are likely to ask is, 'Why did my child have to die?' Generally the emphasis in asking the question is 'Why did *my* child have to die?'

"...There is no easy answer to that question. The answer begins with the fact that life is marked by difficulty and sorrow. We live in a fallen world. We live in a world flawed by disease and sin. Trouble comes to us as part of our human condition.

"...God is omnipotent. He is also omniscient. As a result, some of His purposes and plans we cannot know this side of eternity. God may have allowed a child to die for reasons that will never be understood—reasons that may involve the lives of the parents, the lives of siblings, the life of the child himself, the lives of others unknown by the parents or child.

"There is a question even more potent than the question 'Why did my child have to die?' That question is 'What does God desire for me to do in the midst of this tragedy?' The question of 'Why?' has no satisfactory answer. The question of 'What now?' can turn a person from grief to action, from loss to healing, from sorrow to joy, and from feelings of utter devastation to feelings of purpose."[58]

Privately Address the Theological Reason for Death

Haddon Robinson suggests, "We cannot get into a lengthy explanation of the 'problem of evil' in a funeral message. Theologians have debated this for centuries and still do. The single funeral message is not the place to answer these difficult questions. Later, in our work with the family, perhaps some of these questions should and can be addressed."[59]

The bottom line is that according to Romans 5:12, death entered the world because of man's sin (Genesis 3:14–24). Sin's evil effects (death, pain, suffering, sickness, etc.) will only be banished when sin ceases to exist (after the final judgment). Rightly man ought to place the blame on Satan for the evil of the world, not on God.

Give Assurance That Romans 8:28 Still Stands

God promises to work good out of "all things" for the Christian (Romans 8:28). What a goldmine of comfort contained in this text if one but has the faith to grasp it! God forthrightly promises to use everything that happens to the believer for his temporal and eternal good. He avows to take even the worst that happens and turn it into a blessing.

"No matter what our situation," comments John MacArthur, "our suffering, our persecution, our sinful failure, our pain, our lack of faith—in those things, as well as in **all** other **things**, our heavenly Father will work to produce our ultimate victory and blessing."[60] MacArthur continues, "**All things** includes circumstances and events that are good and beneficial in themselves as well as those that are in themselves evil and harmful."[61]

David echoes the promise of Romans 8: 28 in stating, "All the paths of the LORD are mercy and truth unto such as keep his covenant and his testimonies" (Psalm 25:10).

Make the Sermon Relevant

A death by suicide certainly would demand a different approach than that caused by cancer or an accident. Taking the painstaking time to make the sermon fit the heart need of the family will prove invaluable to them in the comfort and hope received. It is never truer than with a funeral sermon that one size doesn't fit all. Every funeral will have a different fit, so don't try to adapt a "size 12 shoe" to fit a "size 8 foot." Impersonal, stale, and generic messages avail naught in relieving the horrendous pain and sorrow people experience in a difficult death. Resist preaching the same sermon in every funeral. Stay fresh and relevant.

Knowledge Is Power

Understanding the stages that family members experience regarding a loved one's suicide, murder, death by a drunken driver, or accidental death will enhance your preparation of the funeral sermon. For example, following the suicide of a loved one, family/friends (normally) initially experience shock and denial. The next stages include the release of emotions (intense weeping), depression and/or loneliness, guilt, hostility and anger, hopelessness, the slow return of hope, and finally the return to normality and reality.[62]

It is equally beneficial to understand parental reactions to the death of their baby.

- Sixty percent of the parents felt angry.

- Fifty percent of the fathers and ninety percent of the mothers felt guilt.

- Seventy-five percent were irritable.

- Sixty-five to seventy-five percent of the parents lost their appetite, and eighty to ninety percent had difficulty sleeping.

- Ninety-five to one hundred percent of the parents felt a profound and deep sadness.[63]

Accentuate "Afterward You Will Understand"

J. R. Miller in the sermon "Afterward You Will Understand" offers excellent insight with regard to death, especially that which is sudden or unexpected, and that of a child or youth. He states, "But all the mysteries in our lives will someday be revealed. They will not always be inexplicable to us. 'What I am doing, you do not understand now; but afterward you will understand' (John 13:7).

We do not see now how this or that experience can be well and can do good; but after a time, the mystery is explained. The plow cuts mercilessly through the field. It seems only destructive. But afterwards a harvest of golden grain waves where all seemed ruin at first. It is only afterwards that many of God's providences can be clearly understood. It takes time for the full meaning to be wrought out. We do not know in the days of sorrow what 'shining blessing' will be revealed as the final outcome. We do not see in midwinter the roses that are hidden under the snow which after a while will unfold their beauty."[64]

God has given a distinct promise that the mysteries of life will be made clear. Sometimes they are clarified soon, while other times they are left unknown. The fact is that death sometimes occurs without explanation here and now. But another life awaits the believer in Heaven where there is enough time for the deepest mysteries to be made plain.[65]

Review Sermons That Deal with Difficult Funerals

It is proper and advisable to review sermons among other resources from which to gather building material to construct the sermon of the hour. Jim Henry provides such a resource in *A Minister's Treasury of Funeral and Memorial Sermons.*

Other Helpful Hints

For One Murdered the Pastor May Open by Saying

"There is nothing we can say or do today to bring back this life. That is the tragedy of such occasions as this. Nothing will now restore to us the life which has been taken. Our tears will not do it. They can only make us sense our loss more keenly. Punishment of the slayer will not do it. No years of imprisonment can restore the lost years of this man's life. Even the deep contrition of the aggressor will not change the facts. Any words of appreciation which we may say today in honor of the deceased will not restore that life. But there is much that can be done for those who remain [deal with what that might be]."[66] A possible sermon direction would be how God's only Son was murdered, and yet while dying He cried, "Father, forgive them; for they know not what they do" (Luke 23:34).

For Other Tragedies the Minister May Say

"Do we have questions? Of course! We want to ask a thousand whys, don't we? Why did God allow it to happen? Why did he not stop it? We want to know why God allowed sin to come into the world in the first place, don't we? God has answers for our thousand questions. He may give us an answer, or He may not give us an answer, but that does not alter the fact that God knows the answer. God knows what He is doing. We affirm both the reality of a great God and the reality of a terrible tragedy."[67]

The good news is that paradise lost will one day be regained. Evil, though present, is only temporary. Upon Christ's return to earth, evil will be banished, and "the wolf and the lamb shall feed together" (Isaiah 65:25). In Heaven there will be no more tears, sorrow, suffering, sickness, or death. What a glorious day that will be!

A Sudden Death

Death is no respecter of persons, visiting both young and old. No man knows the divine reasoning of God at play in taking someone to Heaven suddenly. "My thoughts are nothing like your thoughts, says the Lord. And my ways are far beyond anything you could imagine. For just as the heavens are higher than the earth, so my ways are higher than your ways and my thoughts higher than your thoughts" (Isaiah 55: 8-9 NLT). Vance Havner underscores the point in stating, "God marks across some of our days, 'Will explain later.'"[68] Until then the bereaved must trust God with the unknowns. "God is too good to be unkind," says C. H. Spurgeon, "too wise to be mistaken; and when you cannot trace His hand, you can trust His heart.[69]

3
Funeral Service

Let the pastor remember that many things he does may be forgotten by his people, but they will always love him for being with them in the shadows of grief.[70]

—Joe Cauthen, former pastoral ministry professor

"The funeral service," writes James Hobbs in *The Pastor's Manual*, "should be characterized by orderliness, simplicity, and brevity. Herein are the secrets of successful and gratifying work in performing this difficult and delicate task. Simplicity without order will leave its unsatisfying impression on the minds of the bereaved, and orderliness without simplicity may irk the bereaved and tire them by its length."[71] Hobbs continues, "The purpose of the funeral service is to calm and soothe the bereaved."[72]

The Request to Officiate

In most cases the family will desire the present pastor of the deceased to conduct the service. Occasionally they will request other ministers to participate.

When Not Requested to Officiate

Regardless of being involved in officiating the funeral or not, attend the service. Respect the family's wishes without taking their decision personally. Exhibit graciousness and humility, giving support to the minister who will preach the funeral message.

Be Courteous to Other Pastors

Upon receiving the request from a family to perform a funeral in another church, it's proper to converse with its pastor for approval.

Do As Asked

In assisting another minister with the funeral, do as instructed. If invited only to pray, just pray. If asked to read Scripture, then don't comment; just read Scripture. The primary officiating minister plays the lead in assigning other ministers their roles and allotment of time. The funeral service is not the time to take liberties which were not given; stick to the assignment. Never agree to officiate at a funeral if asked to lay aside personal biblical beliefs and convictions. In being requested by a family to perform the funeral of a loved one, a pastor was told he could not mention Jesus Christ. Rightly, he refused the invitation.

Casket and Vault Decisions

Should the family request your assistance in casket and vault selections, oblige, but don't take over. Jim Henry cites his approach with such a request: "I try to steer families away from high-priced accessories that family members often have a tendency to prefer because of their desire to honor their deceased loved ones. Some people have the resources to handle this, but many do not. They can be burdened with debt long into the future, and we can help them by encouraging more moderated costs."[73]

Communicate with the Funeral Home Director

Meet with the funeral home director with regard to arrangements (return his/her call promptly). He/she will manage everything outside of the planning and execution of the actual funeral service. Be compliant if at all possible to the day/time of the service, placing the family ahead of personal agenda.

Funeral home personnel are professionals who have vast experience in ministering to the grieving, so don't hesitate to seek their advice if it is warranted. It is imperative that the minister and the funeral director work as a team. Prepare and make the order of the funeral service available to the funeral director as soon as possible.

Family Viewing

Plan to meet with the family prior to the first viewing. This is a deeply emotional time for them which, to some degree, may be relieved by the man of God's presence and prayer.

Visitation

Be among the first to arrive at the visitation to speak to the family. This enables you to become more acquainted with family members and offer support.

Dress

A good rule of thumb regarding funeral attire is to wear a navy blue or black suit with a white shirt, tie, and polished shoes.

Arrive Early for the Service

It's good to plan to arrive at least thirty minutes prior to the funeral service (anticipate the unforeseen such as traffic delays, flat tire, or getting lost). Meet with the family at the funeral chapel/church ten minutes prior to the funeral service in private to comfort and pray in their behalf. The funeral director is well acquainted with the practice and will give assistance as needed. Upon entering the service with the family, ask the congregation to stand and, once the family members are seated, to be seated. At the conclusion of the service, invite the congregation once again to stand as the family and casket exit. Prior to departing the chapel/church, inform the congregation as to the place of the graveside service.

Order of the Service

The order of the funeral service is flexible. The following is a generic, basic order—one that may be adapted. Keep it simple with a time frame not to exceed forty-five minutes.

Instrumental music
Congregational hymn/solo
Welcome in behalf of family and expression of their gratitude for every kindness extended
Scripture reading and prayer (Obituary is optional. I do not use obituaries. All present already know basic information about the deceased. Use the time reading Scripture and ministering comfort.)
Special music

Sermon
Family recessional
Dismissal (Generally the funeral director will dismiss the congregation.)

In the event that others are to assist in the service, assign one to do the Scripture reading and the other to pray. Remarks by another minister might be inserted following the Scripture reading and prayer.

What to Do after the Service

Stay in Touch

Follow up with the family of the deceased after the funeral service regularly for several weeks. Additionally, send letters of consolation to the family on special days such as Christmas, Easter, Thanksgiving, and the birthday of their loved one the first year (and Father's and Mother's Days if appropriate). Place in the hand of each family member a copy of *Grief Beyond Measure, but Not Beyond Grace* (a companion to *The Minister and the Funeral*), which is designed to minister comfort in the pastor's absence.

Financial Remuneration

Upon being asked by the family how much you should be paid for officiating at the funeral, graciously reply, "There is no charge." If the family insists on giving an honorarium, take it. You can always give it to the church's benevolence fund or another such ministry if you prefer. Pastors who must travel great distances to officiate the funeral should be compensated for that expense (airfare, mileage, etc.). In such cases, the funeral director should suggest to the family that such expenses be included in the cost of the funeral. The funeral home, in turn, will issue the minister a check for that amount.

Express Gratitude to the Funeral Home

A note of gratitude from the minister to the funeral home director/staff for an exceptional job performed in ministering to the family is an appropriate act of kindness.[74] In rare cases, such may not be deserved; but for those who go the second mile in making the experience of death as painless as possible for the family, appreciation ought to be expressed.

Ten Things Funeral Directors Want the Clergy to Know[75]

1. Encourage family members to look at the deceased; if they have any hesitation, don't press.

2. Get to know the funeral director, and endeavor to strike up a relationship. Don't shun the funeral director because the kind of work he performs makes you feel uncomfortable; embrace him for his willingness to do it.

3. Return the call from the funeral director as soon as possible. Remember the funeral director is placed on hold until he hears from you.

4. Tell the funeral director the time frame for the service. It's important that the pastor stick to the time frame stated because of other services scheduled based on that time factor.

5. Inform the funeral director of the means of your transportation from the funeral chapel/church to graveside (personal car/funeral home limousine) prior to the day of the funeral.

6. Make the service personal by connecting with the family in sharing stories about their loved one prior to preaching the Gospel. One director shared that he has heard families state following the service, "The service was not about our loved one." Customize and personalize the funeral sermon.

7. The public at large tends to believe that everyone who dies goes to a better place where there is no more suffering. Rectify this error of thought tactfully within the funeral sermon.

8. Refrain from saying "I didn't know John Doe" at the outset of the sermon. Family members already know that, and others don't care. Spend the necessary time prior to the funeral to get to "know" the deceased so that the sermon will come across as if you did know him.

9. Prior to a death, make sure the funeral home director knows the best phone number by which to reach you (cell, home, or church phone).

10. If amplification will be needed in the service (chapel/graveside), notify the funeral director/staff well in advance.

Additional Helps from W. A. Criswell

Keep the casket closed during the service.

Do not open the casket after the service, either at the church or chapel or cemetery.

The bereaved family must not be hidden behind some screen where even the preacher cannot see them. They should be in the front of the main auditorium.

The service is to be held at the church (not meaning a service held in a funeral chapel is unacceptable). "It is just that I think God's people ought to be buried from the church as a last witness and testimony to our commitment to the Lord Jesus Christ."[76]

4

Graveside Service

Don't hold back the tears, and never be rushed. Never will you minister in the footsteps of Jesus more than here. We are His hands and feet. Through us He touches broken hearts.[77]

—John Bisagno

Share with family members upfront that the graveside service duration will be five to ten minutes so they will not be surprised at its brevity. Dress adequately and be prepared for the weather condition (always have an umbrella on rainy days and in wintery weather an overcoat handy). If it is raining or snowing, state at the outset of the service that it is perfectly acceptable for hats or hoods to be worn by all present.

At the graveside lead the casket to the burial plot from the hearse. Once the family is seated and friends are gathered around the tent, read a select Scripture text and pray. In graveside services with two ministers, one may read Scripture and the other pray. Upon completion, either take a step back or give a nod to the funeral director who then will say, "This concludes the service." At that point, move to the chairs where the family is seated to speak to each personally as you pass from the one to the other. At this time, present the departed one's Bible to the closest relative if you preached the funeral message from it. You need not stay until everyone leaves. Mingle among the people gathered at the tent for fifteen minutes or so and leave. Remember to follow up with a visit to the home or a phone call later in the day.

I like to have the Christian flag drape the casket of Christ's soldiers. At the graveside service, at your request, the funeral home staff will fold it and give it to you for presentation to the family.

5
Funeral Scripture

The simplest way to better the average funeral service would be to improve the selection of the Scripture readings. If the pastor chooses aright and reads with distinction, portions of Holy Writ will reach and bless many a heart. What could be more vital? But, alas, the selections are often unwise.[78]

—Andrew W. Blackwood

The following list of selected funeral texts with their themes places at the fingertips of the minister numerous funeral sermon possibilities. Most assuredly, texts cited in one category may cross over into others.

Texts for the Funeral of a Christian

Job 19:23–27—I know my Redeemer liveth

Isaiah 25:6–9—God will swallow up death in victory

Isaiah 26:1–4, 19—God keeps in peace those whose mind is stayed on Him

Isaiah 40:1–10—Comfort ye, comfort ye My people

Isaiah 40:28–31—They shall mount up with wings as eagles

Isaiah 43:1–3a—Fear not...when thou passest through the waters

Isaiah 51:12—I, even I, am He who comforts you

Isaiah 61:1–3—Gladness instead of mourning

Isaiah 65:17–25—Behold, I create a new heavens and a new earth

Lamentations 3:19–26—His compassions fail not; they are renewed every morning

Daniel 12:1–3—Them that sleep in the dust of the earth shall awake to everlasting life

Psalms 23—The Lord is my Shepherd

Psalms 27:1—The Lord is my light and my salvation; whom shall I fear

Psalms 27:4–9a—He will hide me in His pavilion; in the secret of His tabernacle hide me

Psalms 39:4–5, 12—Lord, make me to know my end

Psalms 46:1–5—God is our refuge and strength, a very present help in trouble

Psalms 90:1–10—Lord, Thou hast been our dwelling place in all generations

Psalms 90:12—Teach us to number our days

Psalms 91:1–9—He that dwells in the secret place under the shadow of His wings

Psalms 91:14–16—Seven 'I Will's' of God for the believer

Psalms 116:15—Precious in His sight is the death of His saints

Funeral Scripture

Psalms 121—I will lift up my eyes unto the hills, from whence cometh my help

Psalms 130—Out of the depths have I cried unto Thee, O Lord

Psalms 139:1–12—Whither shall I go from Thy Spirit; or whither shall I flee Thy presence

Nahum 1:7—The Lord is good, a stronghold in the day of trouble

Matthew 11:28—Come unto Me all ye that are heavy laden, and I will give you rest

Luke 23:33, 39–43—Jesus' death upon the Cross; affirmation of life after death to the thief

John 3:16–21—For God so loved the world

John 5:24–29—The resurrection of the dead

John 6:37–40—The promise of Jesus to raise believers up from the dead

John 11:17–27—Death of Lazarus; Jesus visits Bethany to visit Mary and Martha

John 11:38–44—Raising of Lazarus from the dead

John 14:1–6—Jesus' promise about preparing a place in Heaven and returning

John 14:26–31—But the Comforter, which is the Holy Spirit, shall come

Romans 8:14–23—All creation groans for Christ's return

Romans 8:28–39—Nothing shall separate us from the love of God

Romans 14:7-9, 10b–12—Christ is Lord of both the dead and the living/accountability

1 Corinthians 15:3–8, 12–20a—Testimony of Jesus' resurrection/if Christ be not raised, faith is in vain

1 Corinthians 15:20–24a—But now is Christ risen from the dead

1 Corinthians 15:20–26—The last enemy that shall be destroyed is death

1 Corinthians 15:35–44—How are the dead raised up

1 Corinthians 15:50–57—Not all sleep, but all shall be changed; in a moment, twinkling of an eye

2 Corinthians 4:16–5:1—We faint not; we look not at the things which are seen but are unseen

2 Corinthians 5:1–10—For we know that if our earthly house of this tabernacle be dissolved Philippians Philippians 1:18–23—Living is Christ, and dying is gain

1 Thessalonians 4:13–18—But I would not have you to be ignorant, that ye sorrow not

2 Timothy 2:8–13—It is a faithful saying: if we be dead with him, we shall also live with Him

2 Timothy 4:6–8—I have fought the good fight of faith

Hebrews 13:5—   I will never leave you nor forsake you

Revelation 7:9–17—Who are these which are arrayed in white robes

Revelation 14:13—Blessed are the dead which die in the Lord from henceforth

Revelation 21:1–4—And God shall wipe away all tears from their eyes

Revelation 22:1–5—And there shall be no more curse and no more night there

Texts for the Funeral of the Non-Christian

Matthew 25:1–13—But He answered, Verily I say unto you, I know you not

Psalms 39:4–7—Lord, make me to know mine end and the measure of my days

Psalms 1—For the Lord knoweth the way of the righteous; the ungodly shall perish

Psalms 90:12—Teach us to number our days

2 Corinthians 6:2—The right time is now; today is the day of salvation

Hebrews 9:27—It is appointed unto man once to die, then the judgment

Texts for the Funeral of a Child

2 Samuel 12:15–23—Death of David's child; can't bring him back but can go to be with him

1 Corinthians 13:12—Now we see through a glass, darkly

Isaiah 40:11—He shall gather the lambs with His arm and carry them in His bosom

2 Kings 4:26—Is it well with thee; is it well with thy child

Zechariah 8:5—And the streets of the city shall be full of boys and girls playing

Isaiah 11:6—And a little child shall lead them

Matthew 18:1–6—And Jesus called a little child unto Him

Texts for the Funeral of the Elderly

Zechariah 14:7—At evening it shall be light

Job 5:26—Thou shalt come to thy grave in a full age

Psalm 91:16—With long life will I satisfy him

Numbers 23:10b—Let me die the death of the righteous; let my last end be as his

Texts for the Funeral of the Young

Jeremiah 15:9—Her sun is gone down while it was yet day

James 4:13–14—Your life is even a vapor

1 Samuel 20:18—Thou shalt be missed, because thy seat will be empty

Psalms 119:9–16—Wherewithal shall a young man cleanse his way

Texts for a Sudden Death

Psalm 90:12—So teach us to number our days

Job 14:1–2—Man, like a fleeting shadow, does not endure

Psalm 103:15–16—As for man, his days are as grass

Psalms 39:4–7—Lord, make me to know my end

Texts for the Funeral of a Godly Lady

Proverbs 31:10–30—Who can find a virtuous woman

2 Timothy 1:5—When I call to remembrance the unfeigned faith of thy mother

Psalm 35:14—I bowed down heavily, as one that mourneth for his mother

Texts for the Funeral of a Suicide

Psalm 55:5—Fearfulness, trembling have come upon me; horror hath overwhelmed me

Psalm 143:4—My spirit is overwhelmed within me; My heart within me is distressed

Mark 3:28–29—Truly I say to you, all sins will be forgiven

Psalm 69:1–6—The waters are come unto my soul; I sink in deep mire

Romans 8:35–39—Who shall separate us from the love of God

Proverbs 21:2b—The Lord weighs the heart

6
The Funeral Music

As the officiating minister, monitor the type of music selection(s) to be played/sung, making sure they are appropriate. In reference to the selection of music, Andrew W. Blackwood stated, "Speaking broadly, one finds too much about 'death's cold, sullen stream' and too little about the joys of the New Jerusalem. With certain exceptions, the music is neither restful nor uplifting."[79] Song selections should be upbeat and positive, preventing the service from feeling cold and desolate. Blackwood further suggested that organ music be in major rather than minor keys, creating a positive/uplifting tone in the service.[80]

Limit the Number of Songs/Hymns

Special music for the service should be limited to two or three songs—one to open the service and one or two prior to the sermon. Commentary on the song is to be avoided by the soloist, allowing the song to speak for itself. If it cannot, a different song should be selected. Singers should arrive early enough on the day of the service to practice with the organist/pianist or to confer with the funeral director about recorded accompaniment music. The pastor or funeral director must notify the singer upfront of the number of selections to be sung.

In regard to congregational singing, one or two hymn/song selections are sufficient.

The following list of choice hymns/songs for the funeral service is not exclusive. Consider Easter hymns and other songs of Christian hope for additional selections.

Traditional Selections

A Mighty Fortress

Abide with Me

Christ the Lord Is Risen Today

Because He Lives

The Old Rugged Cross Made the Difference

The Old Rugged Cross

Victory in Jesus

When We All Get to Heaven

Precious Lord, Take My Hand

What a Day That Will Be

Beulah Land

Guide Me, O Thou Great Jehovah

I Know That My Redeemer Lives

Joyful, Joyful, We Adore Thee

Love Divine, All Loves Excelling

O God, Our Help in Ages Past

O Love That Wilt Not Let Me Go

The Funeral Music

I Will See You in the Rapture

It Is Well

New Grace

How Great Thou Art

The Midnight Cry

The Holy City

We Shall See Jesus

Amazing Grace

Great Is Thy Faithfulness

Some Golden Daybreak

The Beautiful Place of Somewhere

Safe in the Arms of Jesus

There's a Land That Is Fairer Than Day

Rock of Ages, Cleft for Me

Contemporary Selections

Save a Place for Me

I Will Rise

Cry out to Jesus

Going Home

In Christ Alone

When I Finally Make It Home

The Minister and the Funeral

I Can Only Imagine

The Anchor Holds

We Shall Behold Him

7
Sermon Seeds for the Funeral Sermon

It is highly important, therefore, that funeral sermons should clearly point out the way of life to people and tenderly invite them to Jesus Christ.[81]

—J. A. Broadus

"Man's life is made up of 20 years of his mother asking him where he is going, 40 years of his wife asking him where he has been and one hour at his funeral when everyone wonders where he is going."[82]

With regard to funeral sermons, the minister doesn't have weeks to prepare, but often only hours; therefore, it is wise to have sermon seeds readily available [file] from which to prepare the funeral sermon. The following funeral sermon seeds are offered for such a file.

E. H. Peterson's Funeral Sermon Seed upon the Subject "What Sorrowing Hearts Can Expect from God"

For the bereaved there is always the question, *Why?* Why did this occur? Why did God let this happen? I have found it helpful to focus instead on the question, *What?* What can we expect from God? This concept seems to have therapeutic value for those whom I have counseled.[83]

A Funeral Sermon Seed Thought on Psalm 116:15

Death is not a matter of unconcern to God for either the saint who dies or his loved ones who remain. Yes, "His heart is touched with my grief." The psalmist declared,

"Precious in the sight of the Lord are the death of His saints" (Psalms 116:15). The text is one of the most precious in the Bible.

I. A saint is a person who has been reconciled to God through repentance of sin and faith in the Lord Jesus Christ (Acts 20:21). A saint is a person who has experienced the NEW BIRTH by turning from sin and trusting Jesus as Lord and Savior.

_____ was a saint. He/she was saved, born again to a lively hope in Christ Jesus.

II. Second, a saint is one devoted to Christ. He lives out his faith. _____ did just this.

He/she loved the church. He/she loved the Bible. He/she loved Christian service. _____, though not a preacher, preached many sermons by his/her dedication to Christ and simple service to family, friends and others.

III. Our text calls the death of a saint precious. It's a strange epithet for death, one the world would certainly not ascribe to it, but one so very true. Why is a saint's death precious in the sight of the Lord?

In earlier burial instructions, "Precious in the sight of the Lord is the death of his saints" with other verses was to be chanted.[84]

The practice may not be a bad custom to reinstitute. Why is a saint's death precious in the sight of the Lord? Or to make it personal, why is the death of your loved one precious in His sight?

It is precious due to its freeing power from suffering, sorrow, and sickness. Those who die in the Lord sing, "Free at last, free at last, praise God almighty, I am free at last."

It is precious in that it removes the saint from the present evil on earth and that which is yet to come.

It is precious in that it puts on display the comforting grace of God as a witness to the world of how God sustains His children in the severest trial of sorrow, granting peace and solace.

The death of a saint is precious in the sight of the Lord in that it means he/she is now with Him in Heaven.

It is also precious in the fact that it may be the means of conversion of family and friends.

But saying the death of the saints is precious in His sight indicates that the death of the unbeliever is not. Why? Because at death the non-Christian is forever separated from God and the saints in Hell.

This is not God's desire for you; He longs that you be saved as _____ was, that you may enjoy a relationship with Him today, tomorrow and forever in Heaven! In behalf of our dear Lord and family members, I invite you to receive Jesus Christ as Lord and Savior before you leave the chapel today.

A Funeral Sermon Seed Thought on 1 Peter 1:3

"Blessed be the God and Father of our Lord Jesus Christ! According to his great mercy, he has caused us to be born again to a living hope through the resurrection of Jesus Christ from the dead." Dr. Jerome Groopman wrote, "For all my patients, hope, true hope, has proved as important as any medication I might prescribe or any procedure I might perform."[85] He continues, "Hope, I have come to believe, is as vital to our lives as the very oxygen that we breathe."[86]

Earl Daniels Funeral Sermon Seed Thought on 2 Kings 4:25–26: "The Safety of a Child"

Show the care and protection God gives to children, assuring parents He will keep their little one safe in Heaven until they arrive.[87]

Adrian Rogers Funeral Sermon Seed Thought on Psalm 23[88]

Regardless of the difficulty you may face, I want you to know that there are six verses in God's Word that hold the key to true satisfaction. That's right! Whatever struggle you're facing right now, you can have unshakable peace and contentment by applying these six verses. Where are these verses? Psalm 23.

W. Herschel Ford Funeral Sermon Seed Thought[89]

    I. The Bible says many wonderful things about the death of a Christian
        1. Revelation 14:13
        2. Psalm 116:15
        3. 2 Corinthians 5:8
    II. What does a Christian gain by dying? (Philippians 1:21)

1. He gains freedom
2. He gains fellowship
3. He gains knowledge

III. Lessons for the living (Hebrews 9:27)
    1. Death is certain
    2. The one way to prepare for death

IV. Your comfort in this hour (Matthew 11:28)
    1. You are comforted in remembering you did your best for your loved one (medically, caring)
    2. You are comforted in remembering that death isn't all
    3. You are comforted in remembering that you will see your loved one again
    4. But our greatest comfort comes from Christ

A Funeral Sermon Seed Thought from Billy Graham on I Corinthians 15:26: "Death, Our Final Enemy[90]

The Bible stresses that death is an enemy, not a friend—both of God and of us. Why is death our enemy?

I'm not thinking of death which is a release from pain, debilitating disease, or advanced age, but death the enemy who snatches a child before he learns to play in the sunshine.

It is the enemy who takes the young couple before they can be married, stops the youth who wants to be a pilot, or kills the young father and leaves orphaned children and a destitute wife.

Death like an unfinished symphony leaves fragments of many promising careers and lives.

Andrew W. Blackwood Funeral Sermon Seed Thought on 1 Corinthians 15:53[91]

In the classic chapter about life (1 Corinthians 15), Paul speaks about entrance into the other world as putting on heavenly attire. These words "should help the man in sorrow to feel sure that from a mortal body, with all its frailties and shortcomings, the loved one has gone to be with the Father God."

John MacArthur Funeral Sermon Seed Thought on John 14:1–6[92]

1. You Can Trust His Presence (v. 1). I believe, however, that what Jesus was actually saying is, "You believe in God, even though you can't see Him. You also believe in Me. Keep believing. Your faith in Me must not be diminished just because you will not see Me. I will still be present with you."

2. You Can Trust His Promises (v. 2). He gives them some wonderful promises. "In my Father's house are many dwelling places; if it were not so, I would have told you" (v. 2). That last phrase is filled with significance. He wanted them to know that He was not out to trick them, and He would not allow them to be deceived.

3. You Can Trust His Person (vv. 4–6). "Trust Me," Jesus says. "You don't need a map; I'm the way, the truth, and the life. I am the way to the Father. I am the truth, whether in this world or the world to come. I am the life that is eternal." If your experience is like mine, you've probably had someone give you a complex set of

directions that you could not possibly understand. How much better it would be for the person to say, "Follow me; I'll take you there." That is what Jesus does. He doesn't show us the direction to the Father's house; He carries us there. That is why death for the Christian is such a glorious experience. Whether we die or He takes us in the rapture, we know we can trust Him to take us to the Father's house (John 14:6).

Charles Stanley Funeral Sermon Seed Thought on Psalm 23[93]

In Psalm 23, David compares the Lord to a shepherd who lovingly tends his flock. Through this passage, we learn that Jehovah—the all-powerful, all-knowing, ever present God—tenderly cares for those who belong to Him. Jesus said, "I am the Good Shepherd, and I know My own and My own know Me" (John 10:14). Those who have trusted Christ as Savior have the assurance that He will watch over and nurture them.

1. Jesus is a Personal Shepherd (v. 1a)
2. Jesus is a Providing Shepherd (v. 1b)
3. Jesus is a Pardoning Shepherd (v. 3)
4. Jesus is a Protecting Shepherd (v. 4)
5. Jesus is a Preparing Shepherd (vv. 5–6)

A Funeral Sermon Seed Thought on 1 Corinthians 15:42–53[94]

The resurrection body will be:

1. Incorruptible. Our body now is corruptible, tending towards decay and dissolution, bearing the marks

of injury, disease, age. It becomes more corruptible at death. But the resurrection body will have no such tendencies and be subject to no such influences.

2. Glorious. Our present body is a body of dishonor. The marks of the curse of sin are upon it. In the grave it becomes very inglorious. Paul calls it "our vile body" (Phil. 3:21). The resurrection body will be in striking contrast—a body of glory and beauty, like unto the glorious body of the Son of Man.

3. Strong. Now our body is weak, subject to enervating sickness and when "sown" as a corpse is the very perfection of weakness. But the resurrection body will possess fullness of strength, abundant energy, never diminishing vitality.

4. Spiritual. Our present body is an organism of flesh and blood (v. 50); it is "of the earth, earthy." It is a "natural" body. But the resurrection body will be "spiritual," molded by the Spirit, an organism adapted to the higher and spiritual life.

This poor body we may be glad to lose—certainly its imperfections. But what a life may we anticipate when we are "clothed upon with our house which is from Heaven"! To be free from weakness, weariness, pain, decay, and most of all from carnal cravings and fleshly lusts; to have abounding energy, perfect health, pure desires, and great and completed powers—what service and pleasure we shall be capable of! This is "of the Lord." Is he our Lord? When we die, shall we die "in Christ"?

A Funeral Sermon Seed Thought by C. H. Spurgeon on Isaiah 61:3[95]

Notice with pleasure that in dealing with mourners, according to the text before us, the Lord acts upon terms of exchange or barter. He gives them beauty for ashes, the oil of joy for mourning, and the garment of praise for the spirit of heaviness....I am sure that no mourner would hesitate to deal with Jesus on these special terms, of which only Divine Love could have thought. If you have ashes, will you not be glad to exchange them for beauty? If you are mourning, will you not willingly cease from weeping to be anointed with the oil of joy? And if the spirit of heaviness presses upon you like a nightmare, will you not be glad to be set free and to be arrayed in the glittering garments of praise? Yes, there could not be better terms than those which Grace has invented—we accept them with delight!

A Funeral Sermon Seed Thought on Revelation 14:13: "Death as the Doorway"

1. Death is the doorway to Reception (a welcome Home, my child, personally by Jesus)

2. Death is the doorway to Rest (these bodies get worn and tired, but at death we find rest from the toils and struggles of life)

3. Death is the doorway to Reward (seven potential rewards await the saint; speak of the one(s) the departed will receive, if you know of such, and those every saint should strive to receive)

4. Death is the doorway to Reunion (with family, and friends)

5. Death is the doorway to Release (from sorrow, suffering, sickness, the evil world)

Therefore there is no need to fear its entrance by a loved one or yourself.

A Funeral Sermon Seed Thought by Howard Hendricks on "Scriptural Metaphors for Death"[96]

The Scriptures use three graphic, compelling pictures or metaphors for the death of a believer.

1. It is going to Sleep (1 Thessalonians 4:13–17)
2. It is taking a Journey (2 Timothy 4:6)
3. It is going Home (John 14:1–6)

A Funeral Sermon Seed Thought by Thomas Watson Excerpted from "A Believer's Last Day, His Best Day"[97]

Bernard says, "For Christ to be with Paul was the greatest security—but for Paul to be with Christ was the chief happiness!" When death shall give the fatal stroke, there shall be an exchange of earth for heaven, of imperfect enjoyments for perfect enjoyments of God; then the soul shall be swallowed up with a full enjoyment of God; no corner of the soul shall be left empty, but all shall be filled up with the fullness of God. Here in this present world, they receive grace, but in Heaven they shall receive glory. God keeps the best wine until last; the best of God, Christ, and Heaven is beyond this present world. Here we have but some sips, some tastes of God;

fullness is reserved for the glorious state. He who sees most of God here on earth sees but His back parts; His face is a jewel of that splendor and glory which no eye can behold but a glorified eye.

A Funeral Sermon Seed Thought on Psalm 23[98]

1. The Shepherd is With me (v. 1)
2. The Shepherd is Beneath me (v. 2)
3. The Shepherd is Beside me (vv. 3–4)
4. The Shepherd is Before me (v. 5a)
5. The Shepherd is Around me (v. 5b)
6. The Shepherd is After me (v. 6a)
7. The Shepherd is Ahead of me (v. 6b)

A Funeral Sermon Seed Thought by George W. Bethune on 1 Corinthians 15:55–57[99]

Christian death is before us. The graves are thick around us. There lie many dear—dearer because they are dead. We must soon lie with them.

I do not say, Suffer not—Jesus suffered. Faith teaches no stoicism. But suffer like men valiant in battle, whose wounds, when they smart the most, are incentives to new courage and earnests of future honor.

I do not say, Weep not—Jesus wept. But sorrow not for the Christian dead. They are safe and blest.

I do not say, Shudder not at the thought of death— Jesus trembled when He took the cup into His hand, dropping with bloody sweat. It is human nature to shrink from the grave.

But I can say, Fear not. When death comes, you shall have grace to die. Think of the good who are awaiting you at home in our Father's house; think of the precious ones for whom you weep but who weep no more. Fear not to leave behind you the living, whom you have commended to Jesus; He will remember your trust.

A Funeral Sermon Seed Thought by Robert C. Shannon on 2 Corinthians 5:1–8: "Moving Day"

The one whom we come to honor today lived in a number of different houses. Now she has moved again. That's the way I understand this text. Paul seems to be saying that death is simply moving out of an old house into a new house. In this life we move from one house to another for many reasons. Sometimes the old house has grown too small. Sometimes the old house has suddenly become too large. Sometimes the old house has deteriorated and time has made it no longer suitable. Sometimes the old house is just in the wrong location. There are many reasons, but the basic reason is always the same. The old house no longer fits our needs. The body is a like a house. It suits us well here on earth, but it is unsuited for Heaven! It suits us well in the beginning, but time takes its toll on the house. We are glad, really, that we are not imprisoned forever in these homes. They are too fragile. They are too subject to accident and injury. They are too vulnerable to infection and disease. They wear out too quickly. The muscles grow weak. The eyes grow dim. Even the memory becomes uncertain. There comes a time when it is appropriate to move out of the house of this body into that "house not made with hands eternal in the heavens."[100]

A Funeral Sermon Seed Thought (Death of a Child) by John Bruce on 2 Kings 4:26: "The Shunamite and Her Son"[101]

This story has soothed the spirit of many a [bereaved] parent

1. Though a Godly Person, she was not exempt from family bereavement. She had one on whom her affections centered and who was dear to her, even as her own soul...Whose life seemed indispensable to her own. Yet in accordance with the sovereign purpose of God, she was called to depart with this child. In the morning he is with her....at noon he is struck down by the hand of death.

2. Though a Pious Woman, she was deeply grieved by the loss of her child. When Elisha saw her, he saw grief depicted on her countenance. And why should not Christians grieve the loss of their dear children? It is only when grief becomes immoderate or when mourning is accompanied by murmuring that it is offensive to God. It is chiefly because bereavements awaken sorrow that they lead us to see our need of God and to seek for satisfaction from higher sources than the world with all its transient joys.

3. She Betook Herself to God. The Christian parent should go to God in the season of bereavement.

"He knows our frame," sympathizes, pours the balm of consolation into the wounded spirit.

4. She Acquiesced in the Bereaving, Painful Though It Was. When Gehazi [asked] "Is it well with the child?" She answered, "It is well." True, her beloved child had been removed from her; after a short but severe conflict with trouble, he had closed his eyes in death. And as a consequence...her tender heart was wrung with anguish, and her soul was vexed within her. But still she could say, "It is well."

A Funeral Sermon Seed Thought by Francis W. Dixon on Psalm 116:15[102]

This statement declares that it is the death of a Christian that is "precious," of great value, to the Lord. Why is this? Let us consider four reasons why it is precious to the Lord when one of His children passes through the vale of death.

1. It is precious to the Lord when a Christian dies because the death of a Christian means the homecoming of His child. Jesus has purchased every one of His saints with His own precious blood (1 Corinthians 6:19–20; 1 Peter 1:18–19). This is one reason why all His saints are precious to the Lord, and it is therefore a great moment when they are delivered safely to their heavenly Home.

2. It is precious to the Lord when a Christian dies because death has no sting and no terrors for the Christian (1 Corinthians 15:55–57).

3. It is precious to the Lord when a Christian dies because death for the Christian means the commencement of life in the land of fadeless day. "To die is gain" (Philippians 1:21). How can this be? For one thing, we are so very restricted in these earthly bodies in which we live. We are restricted by sin, and we have to contend with physical frailty. We are being beset by temptations and testings, and we have a powerful enemy who is constantly seeking our downfall. We live in a cruel world, and we experience much sorrow and suffering. In contrast...think of the gladness and the blessedness that will be ours over there in the House of the Lord, for there will be no more sin, tears, sorrow, suffering, or separation when we find ourselves in Heaven. It is not a loss for the Christian to die. The loss is experienced by the loved ones and friends, but to the Christian himself it is gain—a lasting, a perpetual, and an illimitable gain (Revelation 14:13).

4. It is precious to the Lord when a Christian dies because the death of the Christian means a deep satisfaction for the Lord Himself. The time is coming when our Savior "shall see the travail of His soul, and be satisfied" (Isaiah 53:11); in other words, when He shall see some of the fruits of His death and resurrection. What is it that brings satisfaction to His heart? Is it the wonderful thousand years of millennial reign which we are anticipating (Revelation 20:1–7)? Is it the final banishment of Satan and of all evil (Revelation 20:10)? Is it the new Heaven and the new earth that are going to be brought into being (Revelation 21:1)? No, not these,

primarily—but it is the gathering into His presence of all whom He has redeemed (Revelation 7:9–17).

If so, [that you are a Christian] it will be a precious thing to you when the Lord calls you into His presence— but, wonder of all wonders, it will be even more precious to Him!

A Funeral Sermon Seed Thought by John C. Jernigan on "The Uncertainty of Life"

Life has no certainty. It sometimes leaves the body at birth. Life is subject to depart from the body at any time or any age, under any circumstance, and without warning.

1. Man Comes Forth Like a Flower (Job 14:1)

"He cometh forth like a flower." The flower comes forth and is admired by all. It sends forth its fragrance and beauty for a given period of time. The flower has its season; then it fades, and its fragrances disappear. The flower is a wonderful illustration of life; life in its youth and beauty; life during the days of activity; life that is full of usefulness; life that is attractive, talked about, and admired. Such life fades and disappears. Man has but a short season during which he lives. Many never live their allotted time. Man is subject to disappearance at any time.

2. James Compared Life to a Vapor (James 4:14)

Vapor...arises and appears for a little time and then vanishes away (like smoke or mist). No truer comparison of life could be made. Man appears on earth. He is seen and heard for a period of time, but one day he disappears as the mist. He is gone; the world sees him no more.

3. Job Compares Life to a Fleeting Shadow (Job 14:2)

"He fleeth also as a shadow, and continueth not." A shadow is made by an object coming between the sun and the earth. The shadow of a man or tree may be made to flee at any time by the sun hiding itself behind a cloud. The longest life of the shadow is from sunrise to sunset. As the sun drops down behind the horizon, the shadow disappears. Life may flee at any moment and is certain to fade away at the regular sunsetting time of life.

When life is gone out of the vine or stalk that produced the beautiful and fragrant flower, the dead stalk is cut down and moved away. Man is soon cut off, and the psalmist said, "WE FLY AWAY." We disappear; we are soon gone the way that all the generations of the past have gone. Man is here today; he is gone tomorrow. The place to which he goes depends on the preparation here in this life.[103]

A Funeral Sermon Seed Thought by Ian Macpherson on Hebrews 11:4: "The Speaking Dead"

"He being dead yet speaketh."

1. The dead speak to the consciences of the living by their remembered pattern of behavior.

2. The dead in some cases speak to the wills of the living by the challenge of their great achievements.

3. The dead speak to the hearts of the living by the tender recollections they evoke.[104]

A Funeral Sermon Seed Thought on Psalm 46: "The Rope to Hold Onto in Sorrow"

Now precious family members, I want to give you a "rope" which you can hold onto now and in the difficult days of sorrow that lie ahead.

1. It is the comforting Rope of Remembrance

Be comforted in remembering you did your very best for Andy medically and personally. Be comforted in remembering all the joy and pleasure he brought into your life—these memories will ever live in your heart, providing added strength and solace.

2. It is the comforting Rope of Resurrection

A young man's job required his working late at night. Walking home he had to pass through a cemetery, which was terrifying until he thought, *On the other side of the cemetery I can see the light of home and my father is waiting for me.* This forever calmed his heart, dispelling the fear.

On the other side of the cemetery, the Light is on and the Father is awaiting our arrival. And Andy is standing by His side. Death does not have the final say-so about our bodies. God does, and He says, "I am the resurrection, and the life: he that believeth in me, though he were dead, yet shall he live" (John 11:25). Because Jesus has torn asunder the chains of death, being the

Firstfruits of the resurrection, death is defeated, and eternal life is ever the victor.

3. It is the comforting Rope of Reunion

A reunion day is coming with Andy for all who know Jesus Christ. Andy's request was that I share with all gathered here the steps to a personal relationship with Jesus Christ [this I did]. To all who receive Christ as their personal Lord and Savior, as Andy did, I can with all certainty declare you will see him again. You will know Andy then as you know him now. When his child died, David said though he could not bring his child back to this realm of life, he could go to be with him in Heaven. And so will you, with regard to your precious son, grandson, and friend!

4. But above all hold tightly to the Rope of Christ the Redeemer

He lovingly invites, "Come unto me all ye that are weak and heavy laden and I will give you rest" (Matthew 11:28). With open arms He will receive you and grant strength, courage, peace, and hope for this time and the days ahead. He will not fail you nor let you down.

A Funeral Sermon Seed Thought by Jim Henry on Luke 23:39–43: "The Unchangeable Promise of Jesus"

The reality is that all of us will die sooner or later. The questions are, Where will the spirit spend eternity? With whom? And how does one make the essential arrangements? In the unchangeable promise that Jesus gave the thief, we learn that Jesus:

1. Destroys the Idea of Annihilation
2. Denies the Lie of Soul Sleep
3. Declares There Is No In-Between State
4. Demonstrates the Delight of Heaven[105]

A Funeral Sermon Seed Thought by H. Monod on Revelation 14:13

In order to be able to apply the promises of my text, we must therefore die in the Lord.

1. To die in the Lord is, in the first place, to die in the faith of the Lord. It is to renounce all hope of salvation founded on ourselves, on our works, on our pretended merits, and to cause our hopes to rest only on the merits of Christ, on the atonement accomplished by His blood.

2. To die in the Lord is also to die in the love of the Lord. It is to love Him who loved us first, and that unto the Cross; it is to feel ourselves drawn to Him by an intimate and powerful affection; it is, when dying, to be able to say with St. Paul, "I have a desire to depart, and be with Christ, which is far better."

3. To die in the Lord is once more to die in obedience to the Lord. It is to die after having purified ourselves as He also is pure; it is to have lived, I do not say in a state of perfect holiness, but at least in the constant desire of holiness, making continual efforts to reach it and approaching it more and more.

4. To die in the Lord is to die in communion with the Lord. It is to die, after having lived, dead to the world and to sin, with a life "hid with Christ in God."[106]

A Funeral Sermon Seed Thought by F. B. Meyer on Hebrew 2:14–15: "The Death of Death"

Scripture has no doubt as to the existence of the Devil. [Satan's] power was broken at the cross and grave of Jesus. The hour of Gethsemane was the hour and power of darkness. And Satan must have seen the resurrection in despair. It was the knell of his destiny. It sealed his doom. The prince of this world was judged and cast out from the seat of power (John 12:31; 16:11). The serpent's head was bruised beyond remedy.

1. *Fear not the devil, O child of God; nor death!* These make much noise, but they have no power. The Breaker has gone before thee, clearing the way. Only keep close behind Him. Hark! He gives thee power over all the power of the enemy, and nothing shall by any means hurt thee (Luke 10:19). No robber shall pluck thee from thy Shepherd's hand.

2. *Fear not the mystery of death.* Jesus has died, and has shown us that it is a gateway into another life, more fair and blessed than this—a life in which human words are understood, and human faces smile, and human affections linger still. The forty days of His resurrection life have solved many of the problems, and illumined most of the mystery. To die is to go at once to be with Him. No chasm, no interval, no weary delay in purgatory. Absent from the body, present with the Lord. One moment here in conditions of mortality; the next beyond the stars.

3. *Fear not the loneliness of death.* The soul in the dark valley becomes aware of another at its side, "Thou art with me." Death cannot separate us, even for a moment, from the love of God, which is in Christ Jesus our Lord. In the hour of death Jesus fulfills His own promise, "I will come again and take you unto myself." And on the other side we step into a vast circle of loving spirits, who welcome the newcomer with festal songs (2 Peter 1:11).

4. *Fear not the after*-death. The curse and penalty of sin have been borne by Him. Death, the supreme sentence on sinners, has been suffered for us by our Substitute. In Him we have indeed passed on to the other side of the doom, which is justly ours, as members of a sinful race. "Who is he that condemneth? It is Christ that died, yea, rather, that is risen again."

Death! How shall they die who have already died in Christ? That which others call *death*, we call *sleep*. We dread it no more than sleep. Our bodies lie down exhausted with the long working-day, to awake in the fresh energy of the eternal morning; but in the meanwhile the spirit is presented faultless before the presence of His glory with exceeding joy.[107]

A Funeral Sermon Seed Thought Based on John 14:1–6 "The Small Dash on the Tombstone"

(Funeral sermon for my mother, following an evangelistic message)

Jesus said "I go to prepare a place for you." And today we think about that wonderful place that Jesus has prepared for all of us who put our faith and trust in Him. This place is called in the Bible many things. It is called a city. It is called a country. It is called a far better place. This beautiful place is called Heaven. Not a state of mind, nor an imaginary abode but a real, tangible place prepared by Jesus Christ Himself. It is a place in which my Mom resides at this very moment.

I. This Wondrous, Glorious Place Is

   1. A place of Reception by Jesus

   2. A place of Reunion with Saints

Mom is enjoying grand and glorious fellowship with dad and my brother Jimmy, her sisters and all the redeemed of God who preceded her to that city. To see her again you need to be ready as she was to die; receive Jesus as your Lord and Savior.

   3. A place of Release from the Grip of Sorrow, Suffering, Sickness and Sin (Revelation 21:4).

Mom suffered much in recent weeks but now she is free. "Free at last, Free at last, thank God Almighty, I am free at last." God knew what was ahead if she remained and knew she deserved escape from all that and delivered her. Don't we envy her to some degree?

   4. A place of Rest

Mom's continued battle with health issues did not deter her from giving of herself so freely to so many. She refused to quit, working right up to the time she entered the hospital 40 days ago. In the hospital she said to me on at least two occasions, "I am weak, so I need to lean on you for strength." To which I replied, "That's what a family does." But now God has given her rest.

5. A place of Rejoicing Forever

6. A place of Responsibility

II. What Can I Say of My Mother's Life?

On her tombstone it will read, March 1, 1928–January 10, 2011. [The date of her birth with simply a dash representing her life before citing her departure to Heaven.] But oh how much that small dash represents for Mom!

1. It represents her Life of Helpfulness. I don't know of a person that touched as many lives with her good deeds as mom. She so often went or gave or did for others when she herself was sick or in pain.

2. It represents her Life of Humility. She never boasted or drew attention to the good deeds she performed.

3. It represents her Life of Sacrifice. From a child I knew of her sacrificial heart for she oft would do without that her children could have things needed or wanted. And we never ceased being her children in that regard! Race or social status played no favorites with mom; if she was aware of a need she sought to meet it.

4. It represents her Life of Gratitude

5. It represents her Life of Persistence. Don't tell my mom it can't be done for she would do it. This persistence was seen in her battle for life. She experienced setback after setback but kept fighting back. I told her she was stronger than any woman I knew and most men. Indeed she "fought the good fight" to the end.

6. That small dash speaks of the Enormity of Mom's Influence for the Kingdom of God.

I can truthfully say as a child I could but sing, "Jesus loves me this I know, for my mother tells me so." Every sermon I have preached and soul I have won to Christ links back to this godly lady who brought me up in the church and taught me the things of God on "her knees" and help me understand my call to ministry. Lives everyday are being touched for eternity due to her influence upon them. And for sure, "Her works do follow her." Her light will not go out for it shines in so many of us.

7. That small dash speaks of Mom's Love for her Family.

III. What Can Family and Friends Hold Onto in This Difficult Hour?

1. Assurance she is 10,000 times better off with Jesus than in this world

2. Assurance of seeing her again, and that will not be long

3. Assurance from Holy Scripture regarding those who die in the Lord

4. Precious memories of our time with her

5. Knowing that though visibly absent from us her love nevertheless encompasses us

A Funeral Sermon Seed Thought Acts 8:2: "The Ministry of Mourners"

"And devout men carried Stephen to his burial, and made great lamentation over him" (Acts 8:2). Stephen, the first Christian martyr, was carried to the cemetery by fellow believers who engaged in great lamentation [*kopetos*] over him. *Kopetos* refers to grief that is immeasurable. Note, not only did they engage in *kopetos* but "great" *kopetos* for him. Friends who engage in "great" *kopetos* for you and your departed loved one are genuine, the real deal, and will be a source of great comfort if you will allow. "Mourn with those who mourn" (Romans 12:15).

The Sequoia trees of California tower as much as 300 feet tall having very shallow root systems. How do such giants of the forest withstand fierce storms? They intertwine their roots with one another. This is why you generally do not see Redwoods standing alone but in clusters. God uses the deep, solid, rich roots of Christian friends to interlock with ours in the storm of sorrow to strengthen and grant stability. You don't have to face this hour alone.

A Funeral Sermon Seed Thought on Acts 16:25–40: "Saying What He Said"

In the funeral for a suicide, should the family request you to say something that may be of help in keeping others from doing what their loved one did, the following direction might be of help.

Suicide may be prevented by what is said to the suicidal. The Philippian jailer was about to commit suicide when something Paul said stopped him. What did Paul say that changed the jailer's intent? In essence he said, "Things are not what they seem to be; we all are here." "Things are not as bad as you suppose; no one has escaped." "There is a better solution to what you presently are facing, and that is found in Jesus Christ." Dare to intervene with the suicidal as did Paul by saying what he said.

8
Poetry for the Funeral Sermon
I'LL LEND THIS CHILD TO YOU

"I'll lend you for a while a child of mine," He said,
"For you to love the while he lives and mourn for when
     he's dead.
It may be six or seven years, or twenty-two or three,
But will you, till I call him back, take care of him for me?
He'll bring his charms to gladden you, and should his stay
     be brief,
You'll have his lovely memories as solace for your grief.

"I cannot promise he will stay, since all from earth return;
But there are lessons taught down there I want this child
     to learn.
I've looked the wide world over in My search for teachers
     true,
And from the throngs that crowd life's lanes, I have
     chosen you.
Now will you give him all your love, not think the labor
     vain,
Nor hate Me when I come to call to take him back again?"

I fancied that I heard them say, "Dear Lord, Thy will be
     done!
For all the joy Thy child shall bring, the risk of grief we
     run.
We'll shelter him with tenderness, we'll love him while we
     may,
And for the happiness we've known forever grateful stay;

But should the angels call for him much sooner than
we've planned,
We'll brave the bitter grief that comes and try to
understand!"

—Edgar A. Guest

WATCHING AT THE GATE

The little hands are folded like white lilies on his breast;
The busy feet, so noisy once, are evermore at rest.
The snowdrift of his little bed is stainless, smooth, and
still,
As if waiting for the ladle back, his cozy place to fill.

The hobbyhorse is saddled and gives forth a hearty neigh,
But the rider does not heed it, for he is far away.
He is dwelling with the angels, and, though I may be late,
I know he'll not forget me but be watching at the gate.

His toys are laid upon the shelf; his clothes are put away;
The little rug is folded up, on which he knelt to pray.
His empty chair is by the hearth, as if expecting him;
And when I see the vacant chair, my eyes with tears are
dim.

I listen, wait and listen, for a voice that never calls,
For a step along the hallway, but the footstep never falls.
But this comfort I have always, that though I may be late,
I know he'll not forget me but be watching at the
gate.[108]

—Unknown

AFTERGLOW

I'd like the memory of me to be a happy one;
I'd like to leave an afterglow of smiles when life is done.

I'd like to leave an echo whispering softly down the ways
Of happy times and laughing times and bright and sunny
days.

I'd like the tears of those who grieve to dry before the
sun
Of happy memories that I leave when life is done.[109]

—Carol Mirkel

IT IS NOT DEATH TO DIE

It is not death to die,
To leave this weary road,
And midst the brotherhood on high
To be at home with God.

It is not death to close
The eye long dimmed by tears
And wake, in glorious repose,
To spend eternal years.

It is not death to bear
The wrench that sets us free
From dungeon chain to breath the air
Of boundless liberty.

It is not death to fling
Aside this sinful dust
And rise on strong exulting wing
To live among the just.

Giver and Lord of life!
　　　In thee we cannot die;
Grant us to conquer in the strife
　　　And dwell with thee on high.[110]

　　　　　　　　　　—H. A. Cesar Malan

A MAN OF GOD

For fifty years the rostrum
Saw him in that sacred place;
For fifty years the people heard
Him speak the word of grace.
How empty seemed the pulpit
Where his steady feet had stood,
When the messenger from Heaven
Called him up to be with God!

Oh, blessed benediction
Of a life that spent for truth!
Magnificent the mortal
Who served God from his youth!
He has not simply vanished
As a vision that is gone;
Though dead, he still is speaking,
And his light is shining on!

For fifty years he labored
In the Kingdom of the Lord;
For fifty years the people
Watched him live and heard his word.
The house still stands he builded,
Though the toiling hands are gone.

And somewhere God is saying,
"Welcome son of mine—well done!"[111]

—Lon R. Woodrum

THE HANDS OF CHRIST

The hands of Christ seem very frail,
For they were broken by a nail.
But only they reach Heaven at last
Whom these frail, broken hands hold fast.

—John Richard Moreland

THOSE MANSIONS ABOVE

We strain every nerve; we strive for the prize
Of our calling in Christ, a home in the skies.
The battles all fought; the victory won;
We have the reward, "Good servant well done."

Come enter thy home, these mansions above;
Rest in Heaven of infinite love.
From sorrow and sin forever released,
Come sit with the guest at the Heavenly feast.

All stains washed away in robes of pure white,
We bask in His rays; we shine in His light.
The crowns of rejoicing we evermore wear,
The glory of Christ eternally shared.

Make me, O father, more grateful for life,
More willing to bear the turmoil and strife,
More anxious to serve, more like Him to be
Who gave His own life for answer, for me.

That, bearing Christ's image here below,
My work done in him his glory may show,
Fill the summer here in accents of love.
Daughter, come higher and serve Me above.

What glories await the spirit set free
From fetters of earth, untrammeled to be;
The work begins here, is continued above,
And all that's left in life is service and love.

—Anonymous

GOD'S AFTERWARD

God always has an "afterward"
    For every bitter thing.
The flowers may fall, but the fruit abides;
    The butterfly's bright wing
Is painted in its long night sleep;
    Each winter hath its spring.
How glorious is the afterward
    When Easter joy-bells ring!

God always has an "afterward":
    The patriarch Job, of old,
When in the fires was yet assured
    He should come forth as gold.
And Joseph found it thus, when he
    Was by his brethren sold—
A wealth of blessing God designed,
    Unfathomed and untold.

Poetry for the Funeral Sermon

God always has an "afterward"—
       An afterward of bliss;
First night, then the morning, formed the day.
       So must it end like this!
His purpose, higher than our thought,
       We should be sad to miss;
Though hidden, folded in His hand,
       Faith still that hand would kiss.

God always has a shining "afterward"
       For every cloud of rain;
We may not see the meaning
       Of sorrow and of pain,
But nothing God permits his child
       Can ever be in vain;
The seed here watered by our tears
       Yields sheaves of ripened grain.

God always has an "afterward";
       He keeps the best in store,
And we shall see it hath been so
       When we reach yonder shore.
The cross, the shame He once despised
       For the joy set before,
And as we follow we shall find
       Death is life's opening door![112]

                           —Unknown

THE FINAL FLIGHT

Don't grieve for me, for now I'm free;
I'm following the path God laid for me.
I took His hand when I heard His call;
I turned my back and left it all.

I could not stay another day
To laugh, to love, to work, to play.
Tasks left undone must stay that way;
I've found that peace at the close of the day.

If my parting has left a void,
Then fill it with remembered joy.
A friendship shared, a laugh, a kiss,
Ah yes, these things I too will miss.

Be not burdened with times of sorrow;
I wish you the sunshine of tomorrow.
My life's been full; I savored much—
Good friends, good times, a loved one's touch.

Perhaps my time seemed all too brief;
Don't lengthen it now with undue grief.
Lift up your heart and share with me.
God wanted me now; He set me free.

—Anonymous

CROSSING THE BAR

Sunset and evening star,
    And one clear call for me!
And may there be no moaning of the bar
    When I put out to sea.

But such a tide as moving seems asleep,
        Too full for sound and foam,
When that which drew from out the boundless deep
        Turns again home!

Twilight and evening bell,
        And after that the dark!
And may there be no sadness of farewell
        When I embark;
For though from out our bourn of time and place
        The flood may bear me far,
I hope to see my Pilot face to face
        When I have crossed the bar.

—Alfred Lord Tennyson

DEATH CAN HIDE BUT NOT DIVIDE

Death can hide but not divide;
She is but on Christ's other side.
She with Christ, and Christ with me;
United still in Christ are we.

—Vance Havner (regarding his deceased wife, Sara)

SAFELY HOME

I am home in Heaven, dear ones,
        Oh, so happy and so bright.
There is perfect joy and beauty
        In this everlasting light.

All the pain and grief is over;
        Every restless tossing passed.
I am now at peace forever,
        Safely home in Heaven at last.

The Minister and the Funeral

Did you wonder I so calmly
    Trod the valley of the shade?
Oh! But Jesus' love illumined
    Every dark and fearful glade.

And He came Himself to meet me
    In that way so hard to tread;
And with Jesus' arm to lean on,
    Could I have one doubt or dread?

Then you must not grieve so sorely,
    For I love you dearly still.
Try to look beyond earth's shadows;
    Pray to trust our Father's Will.

There is work still waiting for you,
    So you must not idly stand.
Do it now while life remaineth;
    You shall rest in Jesus' land.

When that work is all completed,
    He will gently call you Home;
Oh, the rapture of that meeting,
    Oh, the joy to see you come!

—Author unknown

A WALK WITH SORROW

I walked a mile with Pleasure; she chattered all the way
But left me none the wiser for what she had to say.
I walked a mile with Sorrow, and ne'er a word said she;
But, oh, the things I learned from her when Sorrow
    walked with me![113]

—Robert Browning Hamilton

LIGHT AFTER DARKNESS

Light after darkness, gain after loss,
Strength after weakness, crown after cross,
Sweet after bitter, hope after fears,
Home after wandering, praise after tears,
Sheaves after sowing, sun after rain,
Sight after mystery, peace after pain,
Joy after sorrow, calm after blast,
Rest after weariness, sweet rest at last,
Near after distant, gleam after gloom,
Love after loneliness, life after tomb!
After long agony, rapture of bliss—
Right was the pathway leading to this.

—Frances R. Havergal

SO BRIEF OUR DAYS

So brief our days, so very brief,
Like an autumn rose with its falling leaf.
A moment's light, a glance of sun,
And then our pilgrimage is done.
As the rainbow fades in the summer sky,
As the green grass flourishes to die,
This moment's triumph, too, will wane;
And none shall call it back again.
Write quickly, then, while the candle glows;
A little while and the book will close.
Go carve your figure of renown,
For soon you must lay your chisel down.
Use well this hour's joy, its grief—
For life is brief, so very brief.[114]

—Sybil Arms

SHOULD YOU GO FIRST

Should you go first and I remain
    To walk the road alone,
I'll live in memory's garden, dear,
    With happy days we've known.
In spring I'll wait for roses red,
    When fades the lilac blue;
In early Fall, when brown leaves call,
    I'll catch a glimpse of you.

Should you go first and I remain
    For battles to be fought,
Each thing you've touched along the way
    Will be a hallowed spot.
I'll hear your voice; I'll see your smile,
    Though blindly I may grope.
The memory of your helping hand
    Will buoy me on with hope.

Should you go first and I remain
    To finish with the scroll,
No lenght'ning shadows shall creep in
    To make this life seem droll.
We've known so much of happiness,
    We've had our cup of joy,
And memory is one gift of God
    That death cannot destroy.

Should you go first and I remain,
    One thing I'd have you do:

Walk slowly down that long, long path,
    For soon I'll follow you.
I'll want to know each step you take
    That I may walk the same,
For some day down that long, long road
    You'll hear me call your name.
                      —A. K. Rowswell

THE RESURRECTION MORNING

On the Resurrection morning, soul and body meet again—
No more sorrow, no more weeping, no more pain!

Soul and body reunited, thenceforth nothing shall divide;
Waking up in CHRIST's own likeness, satisfied.

Oh! the beauty, Oh! the gladness of that resurrection day,
Which shall not through endless ages pass away!

On that happy Easter morning all the graves their dead
    restore;
Father, sister, child, and mother meet once more.

To that brightest of all meetings bring us, JESUS CHRIST,
    at last;
To Thy Cross, through death and judgment, holding fast.
                 —Sabine Baring-Gould

I AM NOW IN HEAVEN

I am now in Heaven; the gates have opened wide,
And now I have the privilege of walking by His side.
The angel choir is singing, and the music is so sweet;
I'll join them just as soon as I have worshipped at His feet.

I am now in Heaven, and the blood-washed throng is
    here.
I recognize a lot of them; there's not a single tear.
There's joy beyond description and reunions by the score;
There'll be no separations, for we'll be here evermore.

I am now in Heaven; please wipe away your tears!
I've fought the battle, run the race—I'm rid of all my
    fears.
There is no pain or sorrow here; the heartaches now are
    past;
I've read and sung of Heaven, and now I'm here at last!

I am now in Heaven, and oh, the place is grand!
No one could ever tell me all the beauties of this land.
Since I cannot describe it, you'll have to come and see
That it was worth the trials to live here eternally!

—Becky Coxe

RESIGNATION

There is no flock, however watched and tended,
    But one dead lamb is there!
There is no fireside, howsoe'er defended,
    But has one vacant chair!

The air is full of farewells to the dying
    And mournings for the dead;
The heart of Rachel, for her children crying,
    Will not be comforted!

Let us be patient! These severe afflictions
    Not from the ground arise,

Poetry for the Funeral Sermon

But oftentimes celestial benedictions
        Assume this dark disguise.

We see but dimly through the mists and vapors;
        Amid these earthly damps
What seem to us but sad, funeral tapers
        May be Heaven's distant lamps.

There is no Death! What seems so is transition.
        This life of mortal breath
Is but a suburb of the life Elysian,
        Whose portal we call Death.

She is not dead—the child of our affection—
        But gone unto that school
Where she no longer needs our poor protection
        And Christ Himself doth rule.

In that great cloister's stillness and seclusion,
        By guardian angels led,
Safe from temptation, safe from sin's pollution,
        She lives, whom we call dead.

Day after day we think what she is doing
        In those bright realms of air;
Year after year, her tender steps pursuing,
        Behold her grown more fair.

Thus do we walk with her,and keep unbroken
        The bond which nature gives,
Thinking that our rememberance, though unspoken,
        May reach her where she lives.

Not as a child shall we again behold her,
 For when with raptures wild
In our embracwes we again enfold her,
 She will not be a child

But a fair maiden, in her Father's mansion,
 Clothed with celestian grace;
And beautiful with all the soul's expansion
 Shall we behold her face.

And though at times impetuous with emotion
 And anguish long suppressed
The swelling heart heaves moaning like the ocean
 That cannot be at rest,

We will be patient and assuage the feeling
 We may not wholly stay—
By silence sanctifying, not concealing,
 The grief that must have way.

     —Henry Wadsworth Longfellow

GOD MOVES IN A MYSTERIOUS WAY

God moves in a mysterious way His wonders to perform;
He plants His footsteps in the sea and rides upon the
 storm.
Judge not the Lord by feeble sense, but trust Him for His
 grace;
Behind a frowning providence, He hides a smiling face.
Blind unbelief is sure to err and scan his Word in vain;
God is His own interpreter, and He will make it plain.

     —William Cowper

ANOTHER ROOM

No, not cold beneath the grasses,
      Not close-walled within the tomb;
Rather, in our Father's mansion,
      Living, in another room.

Living, like the man who loves me,
      Like my child with cheeks abloom,
Out of sight, at desk or schoolbook,
      Busy, in another room.

Nearer than my son whom fortune
      Beckons where the strange lands loom;
Just behind the hanging curtain,
      Serving, in another room.

Shall I doubt my Father's mercy?
      Shall I think of death as doom
Or the stepping o'er the threshold
      To a bigger, brighter room?

Shall I blame my Father's wisdom?
      Shall I sit enswathed in gloom,
When I know my loves are happy,
      Waiting in another room?[115]

—Robert Freeman

AFRAID?

Afraid? Of what?
To feel the spirit's glad release?

103

To pass from pain to perfect peace,
The strife and strain of life to cease?
Afraid—of that?

Afraid? Of what?
Afraid to see the Savior's face,
To hear His welcome, and to trace
glory gleam from wounds of grace?
Afraid—of that?

Afraid? Of what?
A flash—a crash—a pierced heart;
Darkness—light—O Heaven's art?
A wound of His a counterpart!
Afraid?—of that?

Afraid? Of what?
To do by death what life could not—
Baptize with blood a stony plot
Till souls shall blossom from the spot?
Afraid?—of that?[116]

—John Stam

9
Illustrations and Quotations for the Funeral Sermon

You don't put enough windows in your sermons. No one can do it better, but you get so interested in your subject, you go on and on with argument and proof texts until the audience is weary. You want to wake them up, let them see out and in through a window—use pointed illustrations.[117]

—D. L. Moody to an esteemed Bible expositor

The dead are the living. They lived while they died; and after they die, they live on forever.

—Alexander Maclaren

Death—the last sleep? No, the final awakening.[118]

—Walter Scott

While death is a decided fact, Death is also a defeated foe. We are able to laugh in the face of Death if we know the Lord Jesus Christ.[119]

—Adrian Rogers

Nothing ever catches God by surprise; He knows everything that's going to happen to us. As the psalmist wrote, "His understanding has no limit" (Psalm 147:5).[120]

—Billy Graham

Death is not a wall but a turnstile.[121]

—Randy Alcorn

"What I am doing—you do not understand now; but afterward you will understand" (John 13:7). Believe this.

Believe that the clouds will lift and that a whole heavenful of sunshine and blue sky will appear! Believe that beyond today's sorrow and out of it will come comfort and joy. Believe that today's stress and strain, pinching and anxiety, will pass away—and that you will have rest, plenty and gladness. Believe that your present burdens will become "wings" to lift you upward into the blessings of eternal life! Believe that the buds under the snow will be glorious roses in a little while![122]

—J. R. Miller

Your pains are sharp. From the pains of Hell Christ has delivered you. Why should a living man complain? As long as you [and your departed loved one] are out of Hell, gratitude may mingle with your groans.[123]

—C. H. Spurgeon

Death is not a blind alley that leads the human race into a state of nothingness, but an open door which leads man into life eternal.[124]

—Martin Luther King

We'll say good night here and good morning up there.[125]

—John R. Rice

We don't own our children. God has given them to us in trust, and normally we spend eighteen to twenty years providing for their training, which represents the period of time we have to fulfill their trust....However, God may transfer our children to His home at any time.[126]

—Billy Graham

Those we love are with the Lord. The Lord has promised to be with us. Now, if they are with Him and He is with us, they can't be far away.[127]

—Peter Marshall

Of course. Of course.[128]

—C. S. Lewis
(on the first words the believer will say in Heaven)

As the much loved Episcopal bishop Warren Chandler lay dying, a friend asked him, "Please tell me frankly, do you dread crossing the river of death?"

The good bishop responded, "My father owns the land on both sides of the river. Why should I be afraid?"[129]

Respond in grief until you find relief. If we bury our grief, it is like toxic waste. It will surface again, and the contamination makes for more trouble.[130]

—Jim Henry

The word *decease* literally means "exodus" or "going out." The imagery is that of the children of Israel leaving Egypt and their life of bondage, slavery, and hardship for the Promised Land. So death to the Christian is an exodus from the limitations, the burdens, and the bondage of this life.[131]

—Billy Graham

Is it right for the Christian to cry? Is it right for the Christian to grieve? Is it right for the Christian to be sad and to weep because of the separation of these who have been taken away from us? The answer is yes. It is right. Christ cried those tears. Paul cried those tears. Simon Peter wept those tears. John wept those tears. The saved through the Bible wept those tears. And we weep them, too. The only thing is this: Paul admonishes us that we're not to cry, we're not to weep, we're 'not to sorrow as those who have no hope' (1 Thessalonians 4:13). Beyond our tears is the triumphant grace of God extended to us in Christ Jesus.[132]

—W.A. Criswell

Joseph Addison, near death, sent for his stepson. When he arrived, Addison said, "I have sent for you that you may see how a Christian can die."[133]

—Robert Shannon

Tears are a natural form of release for the still suppressed feelings of love and gratitude, and also for the reservoir of pain and sorrow we have in our hearts.[134]

—Zig Ziglar

The departures of the saints cause us many a pang. We fret, alas! also, we even repine and murmur. We count that we are the poorer because of the eternal enriching of those beloved ones who have gone over to the majority and entered into their rest. Be it known that while we are sorrowing Christ is rejoicing. His prayer is, "Father, I will that they also whom thou hast given me be with me where I am," and in the advent of every one of His own people to the skies, He sees an answer to that prayer and is, therefore, glad. He beholds in every perfected one another portion of the reward for the travail of his soul, and He is satisfied in it. We are grieving here, but He is rejoicing there.[135]

—C. H. Spurgeon

One thing we can do is not to be judgmental. We do not know what causes a person to resort to taking his own life. It can be burdens about which we had no knowledge or overwhelming tension, anxiety, failures, unresolved guilt, loneliness, or the relentless attack of our ancient adversary, Satan, whom the Bible calls our accuser. It can be a chemical imbalance that, for a period of time, causes reason to be replaced, mental control to be lost, and judgment and the stronger sense of pursuing life to be snapped. We must be compassionate and understanding.[136]

—Jim Henry

Parental comfort may be found in the words Martin Luther uttered regarding the death of his daughter. As his daughter lay dying, Luther with tears asked, "Magdalene, my dear little daughter, would you like to stay here with your father, or would you willingly go to your Father yonder?"

She answered, "Darling father, as God wills." She died in his arms.

As she was laid in the coffin, Luther exclaimed, "Darling Lena, you will rise and shine like a star, yea, like the sun. I am happy in spirit, but the flesh is sorrowful and will not be content; the parting grieves me beyond measure. I have sent a saint to Heaven."[137]

He then said to his wife, "Think where she is gone. She certainly made a happy journey. With children everything is simple. They die without anguish, without disputes, without bodily grief, without the temptations of death, as if it was falling asleep."[138]

All we can lose is the frail tent of this poor body. By no possibility can we lose more. When a man knows the limit of his risk, it greatly tends to calm his mind.[139]

—C. H. Spurgeon

You haven't lost anything when you know where it is. Death can hide but not divide.[140]

—Vance Havner

"Then they who trust in Jesus will God raise up and bring with Him." He doesn't forsake His own. He doesn't leave to perish in the soil and the dust and the dirt of the earth the least of His saints. If He arose, we shall rise, too—crucified with the Lord, raised with the Lord, translated to meet the Lord.[141]

—W. A. Criswell

If you knew what God knows about death, you would clap your listless hands.[142]

—George MacDonald

We shall not know less of each other in Heaven; we shall know more. We shall possess our individual names in Heaven. We shall be known as individuals. You will be you; I shall be I; we shall be we. Personality and individuality exist beyond the grave.[143]

—W. A. Criswell

When Baxter lay a dying and his friends came to see him, almost the last word he said was in answer to the question, "Dear Mr. Baxter, how are you?"

"Almost well," said he, and so it is.[144]

—C. H. Spurgeon

Christ comforts in bereavement by showing us what that which we call death really is to the Christian. If we could see what it is that happens to our beloved one when he leaves us—we could not weep![145]

—J. R. Miller

Heaven is the most marvelous place the wisdom of God could conceive and that the power of God could prepare.[146]

—R. G. Lee

Archbishop Leighton one morning was asked by a friend, "Have you heard a sermon?"

He said, "No, but I met a sermon, for I met a dead man carried out to be buried."[147]

—C. H. Spurgeon

While I will never grow accustomed to life without Ruth, she would be the first to scold me if I didn't look for God's plan for the here and now.[148]

—Billy Graham

It is a period placed before the end of the sentence.[149]

—Carl Jung in reference to the death of a child

We must learn to live on the heavenly side and look at things from above. To contemplate all things as God sees them, as Christ beholds them, overcomes sin, defies Satan, dissolves perplexities, lifts us above trials, separates us from the world, and conquers fear of death.[150]

—A. B. Simpson

My Heaven is to please God and glorify Him and give all to Him and to be wholly devoted to His glory; that is the Heaven I long for. That is my religion, and that is my happiness and always was ever since I supposed I had any true religion; and all those that are of that religion shall meet me in Heaven. I do not go to Heaven to be advanced but to give honor to God. It is no matter where I shall be stationed in Heaven, whether I have a high or a low seat there; but to love and please and glorify God is all.[151]

—David Brainerd

While I am, death is not; and when death is, I am not. Therefore, death is no concern to me.[152]

—Epicurus
[Sadly many embrace Epicurus' view of death.]

God's people live by promises, not by explanations.[153]

—Warren Wiersbe

We love the people of God. They are exceedingly precious to us, and, therefore, we are too apt to look upon their deaths as a very grievous loss. We would never let them die at all if we could help it. If it were in our power to confer immortality upon our beloved Christian brethren and sisters, we should surely do it; and to their injury we should detain them here, in this wilderness, depriving them of a speedy entrance into their inheritance on the other side the river. It would be cruel to them, but I fear we should often be guilty of it. We should hold them here a little longer, and a little longer yet, finding it hard to relinquish our grasp.[154]

—C. H. Spurgeon

Death is not a period but a comma in the story of life.

—Amos J. Traver

Believe me, I am ashamed and blush to see unbecoming groups of women pass along the mart, tearing their hair, cutting their arms and cheeks, all this under the eyes of the Greeks. For what will they not say? What will they not declare concerning us? Are these the men who reason about a resurrection? Indeed! How poorly their actions agree with their opinions! In words, they reason about a resurrection; but they act just like those who do not acknowledge a resurrection. If they fully believe in a resurrection, they would not act thus; if they had fully persuaded themselves that a deceased friend had departed to a better state, they would not thus mourn. These things, and more than these, the unbelievers will say when they hear those lamentations. Let us then be ashamed and be more moderate and not occasion so much harm to ourselves and to those who are looking on us.[155]

—Chrysostom

In death, in the abyss, and in doubt we should remind ourselves, I have the word that I shall live no matter how hard death may press me.[156]

—Martin Luther

I do not know that in Heaven they know all things—that must be for the Omniscient only—but they know all they need or really want to know; they are satisfied there.[157]

—C. H. Spurgeon

You need never ask "Why?" because Calvary covers it all. When before the throne we stand in Him complete, all the riddles that puzzle us here will fall into place; and we shall know in fulfillment what we now believe in faith—that all things work together for good in His eternal purpose. No longer will we cry, "My God, why?" Instead, "Alas" will become "Alleluia," all question marks will be straightened into exclamation points, sorrow will change to singing, and pain will be lost in praise.[158]

—Vance Havner

Death is simply God's angel-in-waiting on the threshold of the unseen to disrobe the soul of its earthly garment preparatory to its passing into the presence of the King of glory.[159]

—R.G. Lee

We measure distance by time. We are apt to say that a certain place is so many hours from us. If it is a hundred miles off and there is no railroad, we think it a long way; if there is a railway, we think we can be there in no time.

But how near must we say Heaven is from us? It is just one sigh, and we get there. Why, my brethren, our departed friends are only in the upper room, as it were, of the same house. They have not gone far off; they are upstairs, and we are down below.[160]

—C. H. Spurgeon

Faith is the vitamin that makes all we take from the Bible digestible and makes us able to receive it and assimilate it. If we do not have faith, we cannot get anything.[161]

—A. W. Tozer

As soldiers, even in peace, perform warlike exercises so that when actually called to battle and the occasion makes a demand for skill, they may avail themselves of the art which they have cultivated in peace, so let us, in time of peace, furnish ourselves with weapons and remedies, that whenever there shall burst on us a war of unreasonable passions or grief or pain or any such thing, we may, well armed and secure on all sides, repel the assaults of the evil one with all skill and wall ourselves round with right contemplations, with the declarations of God, with the examples of good men, and with every possible defense.[162]

—Saint Chrysostom

Hope sees beyond the cloud, beyond the obstacle, beyond the hardship, beyond the weakness, beyond the failure, beyond the difficulty. Hope says to us, "Never accept the verdict of your defeat, the verdict of your melancholy, the verdict of your sickness, the verdict of

your disaster, the verdict of your disappointment. The psalmist says, "Thou hast made me to hope." And Jesus said, "If it were not so [about there being mansions in His Father's House, many of them], I would have told you."[163]
—R.G. Lee

God is sovereign and perfect in all that He does and is. We must recognize that in many situations, we cannot know His full purposes or plan. But we can trust that His purposes and plan are *perfect*. At times we need to remind ourselves of the Lord's words to us in Isaiah 55:8–9.[164]

—John MacArthur

But what about tiny children who do not yet have the physical ability to even know the basic facts of the Gospel or even of any of God's revelation in nature? Does the Bible teach that God will judge them in the same way that He will judge an adult who consciously rejects the truth of God that he knows? No, there are clues that God does not condemn those who are physically unable to know the truth that God has revealed in nature or in the Gospel. One comes from Deuteronomy, chapter one. God is angry because the people would not trust Him to help them take the Promised Land. They rebelled against Him. So he says, "Not one of these men of this evil generation shall see the good land that I swore to give to your fathers [except Caleb and Joshua, who had trusted him]." Then He adds a word about the children: "And as for your little ones, who you said would become a prey, and your children, who today have no knowledge of good or evil, they shall go in there. And to them I will give it, and they shall possess it" (vv. 35, 39).[165]

—John Piper

I once read of the man who lived beside a river but had little interest in the people on the other side until his daughter moved over there to live. I have lived beside the river many years, but this past year [Sara, his wife who had died] has heightened a thousandfold my concern about the other side. I cannot put it into words, but there is an entirely new dimension and a new affinity. Since the dearest to me of all on earth has changed worlds, I am more attracted to that world than this.[166]

—Vance Havner

The measure of a life, after all, is not its duration but its donation.[167]

—Corrie Ten Boom

The Stinger of Death Has Been Removed

A boy highly allergic to bee stings riding in the car with his father became terrified when a bee flew in the window. The father stopped the car, allowing the boy to get out while he caught the bee.

Back in the car, the boy both saw the bee and heard it buzzing and cried out with fear once again. The boy's fear was calmed when the father simply opened his hand revealing the bee's stinger.

Death makes a lot of fuss and noise but is powerless to harm us, for Jesus Christ bore its stinger upon the Cross.

117

The Minister and the Funeral

The Last Words of Augustus Toplady

At age thirty-eight, the writer of the glorious hymn "Rock of Ages," Augustus Toplady, died in London. As death approached, he exclaimed, "It is my dying vow that these great and glorious truths which the Lord in rich mercy has given me to believe and enabled me to preach are now brought into practical and heartfelt experience. They are the very joy and support of my soul. The comfort flowing from them carries me far above the things of time and sin....Had I wings like a dove, I would fly away to the bosom of God and be at rest."

Toplady's last words were, "Oh! What delight! Who can fathom the joys of Heaven! I know it cannot be long now until my Savior will come for me." And then bursting into a flood of tears, he said, "All is light, light, light, light, the brightness of His own glory. Oh, come, Lord Jesus, come. Come quickly!"[168]

A Glad Reunion Day Awaits the Christian

F. B. Meyer in a letter to a friend wrote, "I have just heard to my great surprise that I have but a few days to live. It may be that before this reaches you, I shall have entered the palace. Don't trouble to write. We shall meet in the morning."[169] F. B. Meyer's words echo the sentiment of all who die in the Lord. A glad reunion day awaits with loved ones "in the morning."

Hope Needs a Foundation

A little over a month before he died, the famous atheist Jean-Paul Sartre declared that he so strongly resisted feelings of despair that he would say to himself, *I know I shall die in hope.* Then in profound sadness, he would add, *But hope needs a foundation.*[170]

D. L. Moody's Fear of Death

When it comes to death, some men say, "I do not fear it." I feared it and felt terribly afraid when I thought of being launched into eternity to go to an unknown world. I used to have dreadful thoughts of God; but they are all gone now.

Death has lost its sting. And as I go on through the world, I can shout now when the bell is tolling, "O death, where is thy sting?" And I hear a voice come rolling down from Calvary: "Buried in the bosom of the Son of God." He robbed death of its sting; He took away the sting of death when He gave His own bosom to the stroke.[171]

William Cowper's Suicide Attempts

William Cowper, the great hymn writer (among others he wrote "There Is a Fountain Filled with Blood" and "God Moves in Mysterious Ways") had long struggles with the drive to take his own life. Following 18 months in a mental institution, Cowper was released and met John Newton, who became a great friend. Together they wrote hundreds of hymns/poems.

Cowper nevertheless continued his bout with depression/suicidal tendencies and eventually returned to a mental institution until his death. Cowper's final poem, "The Castaway," was written during that time.[172]

Plan Your Departure

All of us need to make specific plans for our departure from this life. If we don't, we can be left in a predicament similar to that of a young man who became stranded in an Alaskan wilderness. His adventure began in the spring of 1981, when he was flown into the desolate north country to photograph the natural beauty and mysteries of the tundra. He had photo equipment, 500 rolls of film, several firearms, and 1,400 pounds of provisions. As the months passed, the entries in his diary, which at first detailed his wonder and fascination with the wildlife around him, turned into a pathetic record of a nightmare. In August he wrote, "I think I should have used more foresight about arranging my departure. I'll soon find out." He waited and waited, but no one came to his rescue. In November he died in a nameless valley by a nameless lake, 225 miles northeast of Fairbanks. An investigation revealed that he had carefully mapped out his venture but had made no provision to be flown out of the area.

Have you thought about your exit from life? Trusting Christ as Savior and living for Him each day is the only way to be sure we have prepared for our departure.[173]

—M. R. De Haan II

The Last Note Is Not to Be "Taps" but "Reveille"

Winston Churchill planned his own funeral. Selections of the great hymns of the church were to be sung coupled with the eloquent Anglican liturgy. He requested that at the conclusion of the service, a bugler positioned high in the dome of Saint Paul's play "Taps," the universal signal that the day is over. But as Churchill instructed, the moment it was finished, another bugler positioned on the other side of the great dome was to play "Reveille"—"It's time to get up. It's time to get up. It's time to get up to the morning."[174] The last note for the Christian is not "Taps" but "Reveille."

See You in the Morning

In Catherine Marshall's classic biography of her husband, *A Man Called Peter*, she eloquently describes how dark the night of grief can be—and how bright the new dawn of faith. During the summer after Dr. Marshall's death, she returned to the summer cottage at Cape Cod where everything from the boat in the yard to his old shoes under the bed spoke of him. Seeking the solace of the sea, she headed beachward that first tempestuous, lonely evening. As she gazed across the water, she suddenly remembered the last words she had spoken to him. The scene was etched clearly in her mind. Peter was lying on the stretcher just inside the front door, waiting to be put in the ambulance. She leaned over him, and he whispered reassuringly, "Darling, I'll see you in the morning."

Her last line is the best: "And as I stood looking out toward that far horizon, I knew that those words would go singing in my heart down all the years...'see you, darling, see you in the morning....'"[175]

—Paul W. Powell

What Awaits the Saint in Death

A wondrous tale about a boy whose young sister was dying illustrates that which awaits the saint in death. The boy understood that if he could obtain a single leaf from the tree of life in the garden of God, she could be healed. He found the garden and implored the angel sentinel to give him one leaf. The angel consented to do so if he could promise that his sister would never again become sick, be unhappy, do wrong, be cold or hungry, or be treated harshly. The boy was unable to make such a promise. The angel then opened the gate slightly, bidding the child look upon the beauty of the garden. "Then, if you still wish it," said the angel, "I will myself ask the King for a leaf from the tree of life to heal your sister."

After looking upon the wondrous beauty within the gates of Heaven, the boy softly said, "I will not ask for the leaf now. There is no place in this entire world as beautiful as that. There is no friend as kind as the Angel of Death. I wish he would take me too!"[176]

Thought of Death—the Most Essential of All Works

John Climacus, a seventh-century ascetic who wrote "Ladder of Divine Ascent," urged Christians to use the reality of death to their benefit. "You cannot pass a day devoutly unless you think of it as your last," he wrote. He called the thought of death the "most essential of all works" and a gift from God. "The man who lives daily with the thought of death is to be admired, and the man who gives himself to it by the hour is surely a saint." "A man who has heard himself sentenced to death will not worry about the way theatres are run."[177]

Saints Comforting the Bereaved

Queen Victoria heard that the wife of a common laborer had lost her baby. Compassionately she called on the woman and spent some time with her. Neighbors afterward made inquiry as to what the queen had said. "Nothing," replied the grieving mother. "She simply put her hands on mine, and we silently wept together."[178]

Life Everlasting

A pastor in Portland, Oregon broke the news to his congregation that he was soon to die. Then he added, "I walked out where I live five miles from this city, and I looked at the river in which I rejoice, and I looked at the stately trees that are always God's own poetry to my soul. Then in the evening, I looked up into the great sky where God was lighting His lamps, and I said, "I may not see you many times more, but, river, I shall be alive when you cease running to the sea; and, stars, I shall be alive when you have fallen from your sockets in the great down-pulling of the universe.[179]

—Ernest J. Lewis

The Dark Night of the Soul

Writing after the death of his first wife, Martin E. Marty, in *A Cry of Absence*, talks about the wintry season of the heart, the frigid cold blasts that come in the wake of pain or death—an absence in the heart. "Wintry frost comes in the void left when a love dies....The absence can also come, however, to a waste space left when the divine is distant, the sacred is remote, when God is silent." Winter, Marty insists, is just as legitimate a season of the soul as is summer and spring. But it finds little help or understanding. In the current religious atmosphere, only brightly lit summer spirituality is allowed.[180]

—Ronald Dunn

The Anchor Holds in Spite of the Storm

Hebrews 6:18–19 is an analogy of olden days when most ships had sails. When such a ship approached a harbor difficult to navigate, the captain would send a seaman ahead in a small boat with the anchor attached to a rope that extended back to the ship. Once in the bay, the seaman would drop the anchor. The captain then would give orders to the crew to pull the rope little by little, drawing the ship safely into the harbor. In the Christian life, Christ has gone before us to drop the anchor within the harbor of Heaven.[181] The anchor is Scripture, God's promises, all of which insure security, strength and stability amidst life's storms until life's journey ends in the harbor of the Celestial City.

Story Behind "It Is Well with My Soul"

Horatio Spafford and his family decided to join the D. L. Moody team on an evangelistic crusade in Europe. Spafford's wife and four daughters departed without him; he was to join them in a week. Tragically, the ship on which they were sailing collided with another vessel and sank within twenty minutes. Spafford's wife, Anna, was the only family survivor. Ten days later from the hospital Anna sent her husband a message that consisted of two words: "Saved alone."

He was devastated and shook uncontrollably. Major Whittle, Spafford's friend, consoled him and traveled with him to France to see his wife. En route, the captain awoke him at the spot where his children drowned, as he requested. Upon looking into the dark, cold water that now was their grave, he wept. He then sat down and penned the words of a hymn that has brought comfort and hope to many in their hour of grief.

He Has Gone, He Has Come

You watch a ship move out of the harbor, and you say, "It's going." You watch it sink below the horizon, and you say, "It's gone." But on another shore there are those who are watching for this same ship on some other day. Soon they see the smoke, then the funnels, then the hull. And they say, "It's coming." As it pulls into port, they say, "It's here." In like manner, we stand by the deathbeds of our loved ones. We say, "He is going." As he breathes his last, we say, "He has gone." But there are watchers on some other shore who say, "He has come. He is home at last." Yes, death is just a departure.[182]

—Herschel Ford

All Is Well

Robert Louis Stevenson tells the story of a ship that was caught in a terrific storm, threatening the lives of its passengers. Against orders, one passenger braved the storm to get to the pilot's house. He observed the steersman at his post steadily holding the wheel, turning it inch by inch, and turning the ship back to sea. The pilot, seeing the passenger, smiled. The daring passenger, upon returning below deck where others awaited, said cheerfully, "I have seen the face of the pilot, and he smiled. All is well."[183] Amidst the voracious storms of sorrow pounding the ship of your life, its Pilot is smiling, giving assurance all will be well.

A Lesson from the Grieving Caterpillars

Cartoonist Arthur Brisbane pictured a crowd of grieving caterpillars carrying the corpse of a cocoon to its final resting place. The poor, distressed caterpillars, attired in black clothing, were weeping and greatly distraught at the death of their friend. But all the while, their friend, now a beautiful butterfly, fluttered happily above them, totally free from its earthly shell. To the grieving caterpillars, his death was mysterious and saddening; but to him it was glorious, freeing and exhilarating.[184]

Death Is Not a Period but a Comma

"Death is not a period but a comma in the story of life" (Amos J. Traver). In English grammar, a period at the conclusion of a sentence means "the end; nothing more is coming; the thought has been completed." In contrast, a comma loudly states, "Take a breath; relax a moment. Get prepared, for there is more to come." What a wonderful description of death! Death is not a period to one's life, only a comma indicating "the best is yet to be."

Life Is Swift

You will find its swiftness spoken of in the Book of Job, where we are furnished with three illustrations. First, life is swifter than a post (Job 9:25). In ancient days, monarchs received speedy intelligence reports by post—swift horses and constant relays that was a marvel of that day. Job states our days are swifter than a post—not like the slow wagon that drags along the road, but like a post attaining great speed. It passes rapidly. Second, life passes away as the swift ships (Job 9:26). The metaphor of the rapid flow of life is increased. Swift are the ships, but swifter far is life. Third, life is "as the eagle that hasteth to the prey." The eagle is known for its speed. Its swiftness is incalculable. Now you see it; now you don't. Job states life is like the swiftness of an eagle. "It is like an eagle hasting to its prey—not merely an eagle flying in its ordinary course, but an eagle hasting to its prey. Life appears to be hasting to its end; death seeks the body as its prey. Life is ever fleeing from insatiate death, but death is too swift to be outrun; and as an eagle overtakes its prey, so shall death.[185]

—C. H. Spurgeon

The tapestry of death

When you look at the back of a tapestry, you see many colored threads in a maze of confusion. But when you turn the tapestry over, you see all the colors gathered together and blended into a beautiful picture. Today we are looking at the back side of the weaving. There are some black threads mingled with the others, and we see no beauty there. But someday, when we are with Jesus, we will see that God was working everything together for good and His glory. You who loved this little one cannot see this now, but I am sure that you will see it in the sweet by-and-by.[186]

—Herschel Ford

Appointment in Samarra (Death Is Inescapable)

[The speaker is Death] There was a merchant in Bagdad who sent his servant to market to buy provisions. In a little while the servant came back, white and trembling, and said, "Master, just now when I was in the marketplace I was jostled by a woman in the crowd, and when I turned, I saw it was Death that jostled me. She looked at me and made a threatening gesture. Now, lend me your horse, and I will ride away from this city and avoid my fate. I will go to Samarra, and there Death will not find me." The merchant lent him his horse, and the servant mounted it. He dug his spurs in its flanks, and as fast as the horse could gallop, he went.

Then the merchant went down to the marketplace, and he saw me standing in the crowd. He came to me and said, "Why did you make a threatening gesture to my servant when you saw him this morning?"

"That was not a threatening gesture," I said. "It was only a start of surprise. I was astonished to see him in

Baghdad, for I had an appointment with him tonight in Samarra.[187]

—W. Somerset Maugham

Sing in the Night of Sorrow

Charles Haddon Spurgeon preached a sermon on "Songs in the Night" (see Job 35:10). He gave reasons why we should sing in the night.

One was that others who travel the same dark way will hear, find guidance, and receive strength. So in your night of bereavement—sing! Sing for your own welfare and for that of others. In so doing you will find help for the night and assurance for the day that soon will dawn.[188]

A Picture: "And That Is Death"

I stand upon the seashore. A ship at my side spreads her white sails to the morning breeze and moves softly out to the blue ocean. She is an object of beauty and strength. I stand and look at her until at length she hangs like a speck of white cloud just where the sea and sky come down to mingle with one another.

Then someone at my side exclaims, "Look, she's gone!"

Gone where? Gone from my sight, that is all. She is just as large in mast and hull as she ever was. Her diminished size lies in me, not her. And at the very moment when someone at my side exclaims, "Look, she's gone!" there are other eyes eagerly watching her approach and other voices ready to take up the glad shout, "Look, she's coming home!"

And that is death.

—Anonymous

A White Soul

When the poet Henry Wadsworth Longfellow lay in the dignity of death, his friend, Ralph Waldo Emerson, whose memory was failing, came to pay his respects. Standing by the casket, unable to identify him, Emerson, speaking slowly and calmly, said, "I don't remember this gentleman's name, but he was a white soul."[189]

Epitaph of a Dentist Named John Brown

Stranger! Approach this spot with gravity!
John Brown is filling his last cavity.[190]

Epitaph on the Tombstone of Solomon Peas, London, England

Beneath these clouds and beneath these trees
Lies the body of Solomon Peas.
This is not Peas; it is only his pod.
Peas has shelled out and gone Home to God.[191]

Epitaph of a Watchmaker at St. Petrock's Church, Lyford, Devon, England

Here lies in horizontal position the outside case of dear George Routleight, watchmaker, whose abilities in that line were an honour to his profession—integrity was the mainspring and prudence the regulator of all the actions of his life. Humane, generous, and liberal, his hand never stopped until he had relieved distress. So nicely regulated were all his movements that he never went wrong, except when set agoing by people who did not know his key; even then he was easily set right again. He had the art of disposing his time so well that the hours glided away in one continued round of pleasure and delight, till an unlucky moment put a period to his existence. He departed this life November 14, 1802, aged fifty-seven. Wound up in hopes of being taken in hand by his Maker and being thoroughly cleansed, repaired, and set agoing in the world to come.[192]

How Many Sundays?

The late Leslie Weatherhead told of being called to see a dying man who was afraid to die. As London's great preacher visited with the stranger about God, the church, Christ, and things of the Spirit, the man replied, "I have been too busy for these things. I have never had time."

Weatherhead concluded his story by saying, "The man had been permitted to live four thousand Sundays!"[193]

Arrived

There are Christians of a certain tribe in Africa who never say of their dead "who die in the Lord" that "they have departed!" Speaking, as it were, from the vantage point of the Gloryworld, they triumphantly and joyously say, "They have arrived!" What joy, even in sorrow, is ours when we say of our loved ones who enter life eternal trusting Jesus: "Absent from the body—at home with the Lord!"

—Walter Knight

You Need Not Tell Me

Sir Francis Newport, the head of an English infidel club, said to those gathered around his dying bed, "You need not tell me there is no God, for I know there is one and that I am in His angry presence! You need not tell me there is no Hell, for I already feel my soul slipping into its fires! Wretches, cease your idle talk about there being hope for me! I know I am lost forever."[194]

How Happy the Angels Will Be

Phillips Brooks, the writer of "O Little Town of Bethlehem," was one of the greatest pulpit orators and best-loved preachers of the 19th century.

No greater tribute could be paid him than the words of a five-year-old Boston girl, who exclaimed after her mother had told her that the beloved Mr. Brooks had died, "Mother, how happy the angels will be!"[195]

Certainties

When the great Christian and scientist, Sir Michael Faraday, was dying, some journalists questioned him as to his speculations about life after death.

"Speculations!" he said, "I know nothing about speculations. I'm resting on certainties. 'I know that my redeemer liveth, and because He lives, I shall live also.'"[196]

Waterbugs and Dragonflies Story by Doris Stickney

Rainbow Bridge.com has a great story for explaining death to children. It is called "Waterbugs and Dragonflies" and can be found at the web address located in the endnotes.[197]

Ascended

In a London cemetery is a grave with a headstone with very unusual but beautiful wording. It was erected by the famous pastor Joseph Parker for his beloved wife. He could not bring himself to write the word "Died" and instead chose the better word "Ascended." When he himself passed away, his friends had his headstone carved with the following inscription: "Joseph Parker, Born April 9, 1830, Ascended November 28, 1902."[198]

Reach Out and Touch God

Many years ago, Benjamin Harrison who later became the twenty-third president of the United States was asked to deliver an address at a funeral service. When he arose to speak, he said, "Last night I was awakened by my little daughter who had arisen from her bed and made her way across the room and was stroking my face with her chubby hands. When I asked what she wanted, she said, 'Papa, in the great big dark of the night I am lonely and afraid unless I can touch you....' In the great big dark of the night of life's bereavement, we are afraid unless we can reach out and touch God." The land beyond the grave is dark, and we would be afraid if we could not, by faith in Jesus, reach out and touch the Father. But we can. And when we do, we no longer are afraid.[199]

—Paul W. Powell

The Boy and the Bridge

A father's business required him to take a long walk through the Alps early in the morning and back home after dark. As his son grew up, he begged to be taken on these trips, but the father thought his little legs too weak to make the journey. Finally, after years of refusal, the father gave in and agreed to take him on the next trip. In the early morning walk, they crossed a high rope bridge, with a few missing slats, suspended over the valley. With daylight and dad leading the way, it posed no problem for the young boy to cross. Once completing their business in the city, they set out for home. The boy began to worry about crossing the rope bridge at dark and shared that fear with his father. The missing slats, the deep gorge, the thick darkness all were of grave concern. Unable to cross the bridge until they came to it, the father was unable to give the boy assurance that everything would be just fine. With strong arms and a loving heart, he placed his son on his back seeking to assure him.

The next thing the boy remembered was awaking to early rays of sunlight and seeing a silhouette of his father standing in the doorway. "Dad, what happened?" the boy inquired. "What about the bridge?" he worried out loud.

"Well, son, you fell asleep with your arms around my neck. I carried you across the bridge and laid you safely laid in your own bed. You've just awakened on the other side."[200] What a beautiful picture of the death of a child of God!

Our Lord Reigns

David Watson was the dynamic pastor of the St. Michael's Church in York, England. Large crowds filled the sanctuary week after week to hear him call them to faith and fellowship with Jesus. In the prime of his life, Watson was diagnosed with cancer. The people prayed, and he fought it. But, in the end, it ravaged his body, and he went home to the Chief Bishop of his soul.

The following Sunday, a cherished friend was asked to lead in the worship and the communion service. When he stood to speak, emotion overcame him as he thought of the absence of his recently deceased friend. He wept, as did the grief-stricken congregation. Then someone thought about a phrase that David often used. Sometimes, even in the middle of a message, Watson would shout, "Our Lord reigns!" Quietly, but strongly enough to be heard, he said, "Our Lord reigns." Another picked it up. Then another joined them. Soon the packed sanctuary was filled with hundreds of voices, chanting together on their feet, "Our Lord reigns!" For minutes, it rocked the cavernous worship hall. Applause and cheering broke out. Depression gave way to celebration. The Sovereign of the Sudden was, is, and always will be in charge. In our pain and sorrow, we stand on the everlasting truth, "Our Lord reigns!"[201]

—Jim Henry

Home Safe at Last

A Christian railroad engineer was speaking to a group of fellow workers about Heaven. He said, "I can't begin to tell you what the Lord Jesus means to me. In Him I have a hope that is very precious. Let me explain.

"Many years ago as each night I neared the end of my run, I would always let out a long blast with the whistle just as I'd come around the last curve. Then I'd look up at the familiar little cottage on top of the hill. My mother and father would be standing in the doorway waving to me. After I had passed, they'd go back inside and say, 'Thank God, Benny is home safe again tonight.' Well, they are gone now, and no one is there to welcome me. But someday when I have finished my 'earthly run' and I draw near to Heaven's gate, I believe I'll see my precious mother and dad waiting there for me. And the one will turn to the other and say, 'Thank God, Benny is home safe at last.'"

—Source Unknown

What's Beyond the Door?

A dying man asked his Christian doctor to tell him something about the place to which he was going. As the doctor fumbled for a reply, he heard a scratching at the door, and he had his answer. "Do you hear that?" he asked his patient. "It's my dog. I left him downstairs, but he has grown impatient and has come up and hears my voice. He has no notion what is inside this door, but he knows that I am here. Isn't it the same with you? You don't know what lies beyond the Door, but you know that your Master is there."[202]

—A. M. Hunter

ENDNOTES

[1] Wiersbe, Warren W. and David W. Wiersbe. *Comforting the Bereaved*. (Chicago: Moody Publishers, 1985), 6.

[2] Ironside, H. A. *Illustrations of Bible Truth*. (Chicago: Moody Press, 1945), Foreword.

[3] Blackwood, Andrew W. *The Funeral: A Source Book for Ministers*. (Philadelphia: Westminster Press, 1977), 14.

[4] Gibson, Scott M. *Preaching for Special Services*. (Grand Rapids: Baker Books, 2001), 43.

[5] Wiersbe, Warren. *The Dynamics of Preaching*. (Grand Rapids: Baker Books, 1999), 125.

[6] Bisagno, John and Rick Warren. *Letters to Timothy* (Nashville: B and H Publishers, 2001), 95.

[7] Peterson, E. H. and C. Miller. (1987). *Vol. 10: Weddings, funerals, & special events*. The Leadership Library (93). Carol Stream, IL; Waco, TX: Christianity Today, Inc.; Word Books.

[8] Broadus, J. A. *A Treatise on the Preparation and Delivery of Sermons* (23rd edition, E. C. Dargan, Ed.). (New York: A. C. Armstrong and Son, 1898), 103.

[9] Spurgeon, C. H. "I Know That My Redeemer Liveth." http://www.spurgeon.org/sermons/0504.htm, accessed July 27, 2013.

[10] http://www.goodreads.com, accessed August 13, 2013.

[11] Criswell W. A. *Criswell's Guidebook for Pastors.* (Nashville: Broadman Press, 1980), 298.

[12] Oates, Wayne. *Grief, Transition and Loss.* (Minneapolis: Augsburg Press, 1997), 14.

[13] Powell, Paul W. *The New Minister's Manual.* (Waco: George W. Truett Theological Seminary, 1994), 28.

[14] Conwell, Russell H. *One Thousand Thoughts for Funeral Occasions,* (New York: Harper & Brothers, 1912), Publisher's Foreword.

[15] Segler, Franklin M. *A Theology of Church and Ministry.* (Nashville: Broadman Press, 1960), 182. Maclaren continued to say, "Unless that be our bond, the sooner these walls crumble and this voice ceases and these pews are emptied the better."

[16] Blackwood, 136–137

[17] Reeder, Harry. "The Pastor and the Funeral," (Tabletalk Magazine, October 1, 2011). http://www.ligonier.org, accessed May 17, 2013.

[18] Biddle, Perry H., Jr., *A Funeral Manual.* (Grand Rapids: Wm. B. Eerdmans Publishing Co., 1994), 32.

[19] "Ten Commandments for Preaching a Funeral," (Preachers Magazine). www.nazarenepreacher.org, accessed May 16, 2013.

[20] Broadus, 304.

[21] Hughes, Robert G. *A Trumpet in Darkness: Preaching to Mourners*. (Philadelphia: Fortress Press, 1985), 10.

[22] Broadus, 248.

[23] Powell, 25.

[24] Hughes, 88.

[25] Criswell, *Guidebook for Pastors*, 297.

[26] Edwards, Tryon. *A Dictionary of Thoughts: Being a Cyclopedia of Laconic Quotations from the Best Authors of the World, Both Ancient and Modern*. (Detroit: F. B. Dickerson Co., 1908), 543.

[27] Spurgeon, C. H. *Lectures to My Students*. (Grand Rapids: Zondervan, 1970), 135.

[28] Broadus, 304.

[29] Malphurs, Aubrey and Keith Willhite. *A Contemporary Handbook for Weddings and Funerals*. (Grand Rapids: Kregel Publications, 2003), 212.

[30] Spurgeon, *Lectures to My Students,* 86.

[31] Blackwood, 140–141.

[32] Duduit, Michael, ed. *Handbook of Contemporary Preaching*. (Nashville: Broadman Press, 1992), 163.

[33] Ironside, Foreword.

[34] ibid.

[35] Robinson, Haddon W. "What is Expository Preaching?" *Bibliotheca Sacra* 131, (January–March, 1974), 57.

[36] Stott, J. R. *Preacher's Portrait*. (London: Tyndale Press, 1961), 25.

[37] Braga, James. *How to Prepare Bible Messages*. (Sisters, Oregon: Multnomah Publishers, Inc., 2005), 37.

[38] Barlow, Jerry N. "The Expositional Eulogy: Teaching Pastoral Preaching for Funeral Sermons," http://www.ehomiletics.com/papers/03/Barlow2003.pdf, p. 4, accessed May 26, 2013. (In the appendix of this article an example of the expositional eulogy is shared.)

[39] Douglas, J. D., ed. *The Work of the Evangelist*. (Minneapolis: World Wide Publications, 1984), 776.

[40] Barth, Karl. *Homiletics*. (Louisville: Westminster John Knox Press, 1991), 49.

Endnotes

---

[41] Daniels, Earl. *The Funeral Message*. (Nashville: Cokesbury, 1937), 19.

[42] Hughes, 9.

[43] Spurgeon, C. H. *The Mourner's Comforter*. (Columbia, Maryland: Opine Publishing, 2007), 15–16.

[44] ibid.

[45] http://www.thefreedictionary.com/eulogy, accessed May 30, 2013.

[46] Bisagno and Warren, 100.

[47] Bryant, James W., Mac Brunson. *The New Guidebook for Pastors*. (Nashville: The B and H Publishing Group, 2007), 153.

[48] Henry, Jim. *A Minister's Treasure of Funeral and Memorial Messages*. (Nashville: Broadman and Holman, 2003), 6.

[49] Browning, Robert. "Rabbi Ben Ezra." In *Immortal Poems of the English Language*, edited by Oscar Williams. (New York: Washington Square Press, 1952), 400.

[50] Merriam-Webster Dictionary.

[51] Gangel, K. O. *Holman New Testament Commentary, Vol. 5: Acts*. (Nashville: Broadman & Holman Publishers, 1998), 421–422.

52 Powell, 23.

53 Daniels, 103–108.

54 Chappell, Bryan. *The Hardest Sermons You'll Ever Have to Preach.* (Grand Rapids: Zondervan, 2011), 14.

55 Peterson and Miller, 129.

56 Chappell, 244–250.

57 Herrod, Dr. Ron. Personal correspondence, August 16, 2013.

58 MacArthur, John. *Safe in the Arms of God.* (Nashville: Thomas Nelson , 2003), 133–134.

59 ibid.

60 MacArthur, John. *The MacArthur New Testament Commentary: Romans, Vol. 1.* (Chicago: Moody Press, 1991), 473.

61 ibid.

62 Shivers, Frank. *Hot Buttons on Morality*. (La Vergne, Tennessee: Lighting Source, 2013), 63–64.

63 Cullberg, J. "Mental Reactions to Women to Perinatal Death" from *Psychosomatic Medicine in Obstetrics and Gynecology*, ed. N. Morris. (Basel: S. Karger, 1971).

Endnotes

Miller, J . R. "Afterward You Will Understand" (sermon, 1909), http://www.gracegems.org/Miller/afterward_you_will_underst and.htm, accessed August 15, 2013.

Daniels, 63.

Benton, Wilson, cited by Chappell, 248.

Morgan, R. J. *Nelson's Complete Book of Stories, Illustrations, and Quotes* (electronic ed.). (Nashville: Thomas Nelson Publishers, 2000), 767.

"Who wrote, 'Our Father is too wise to be mistaken; our Father is too good to be unkind, so when you can't see his plan, when you can't trace his hand, trust His heart?'" wiki.answers.com.

Cothen, Joe H. Equipped for Good Work: A Guide for Pastors. 2d ed. Revised by Joe H. Cothen and Jerry N. Barlow. (Gretna: Pelican, 2002), 166.

Hobbs, James R. *The Pastor's Manual*. (Nashville: Broadman Press, 1962), under heading "Notes on Conducting a Funeral.

Henry, 5.

Blackwood, 184.

[75] Personal correspondence from Tommy Murrow, Joe Burns Funeral Homes, Perry, Florida, May 22, 2013, with other sources adapted.

[76] Criswell, *Guidebook for Pastors*, 299.

[77] Bisago, John R. and Rick Warren. *The Pastor's Handbook*. (Nashville: B and H Books, 2011), 124.

[78] Blackwood, 89.

[79] ibid., 87–89.

[80] ibid., 93.

[81] Broadus, 303–304.

[82] Sermon Builder. http://www.timothyreport.com/funeral.html, accessed May 30, 2013.

[83] Peterson and Miller, 84–85.

[84] Lockyer, Herbert. *The Death of the Saints* in *The Sword of the Lord*. (Murfreesboro, TN: Sword of the Lord Publishers, March 29, 2013), 11.

[85] Groopman, Jerome. *The Anatomy of Hope*. (New York: Random House, 2004), 14.

[86] ibid., 208.

[87] Daniels, 63.

[88] Rogers, Adrian. *The Secret of Satisfaction.* http://www.lwf.org, accessed May 12, 2013.

[89] Ford, Hershel. *Simple Sermons for Funeral Services.* (Grand Rapids: Zondervan, 1962), 11–16. [Helpful resource for funeral sermon preparation on the spare of the moment]

[90] Graham, Billy. *Death and the Life After.* (Nashville: W Publishing Group, 1987), 6.

[91] Blackwood, 141.

[92] MacArthur, John. "The Solution to a Troubled Heart." http://www.gty.org, accessed May 22, 2013.

[93] Stanley, Charles. "The Lord—Our Shepherd." www.intouch.org, accessed May 14, 2013.

[94] Spence-Jones, H. D. M., Ed. *The Pulpit Commentary: 1 Corinthians.* (London; New York: Funk & Wagnalls Company, 1909), 538.

[95] Spurgeon, *The Mourner's Comforter,* 74.

[96] Malphurs and Willhite, 167–173.

[97] http://www.christianitytoday.com/ch/thepastinthepresent/ classicfaithformoderntimes/abelieverslastday.html? start=1, accessed May 22, 2013.

[98] Unknown source.

[99] Meyer, F. B., C. H. Spurgeon, Albert Barnes, and Others. *Funeral Sermons and Outlines.* (Grand Rapids:Baker Book House, 1955), 44–45.

[100] Shannon, Robert C. *The Minister's Manual.* (New York: HarperFrancisco, 1990), 27.

[101] ibid., 66–67. (Abbreviated from original)

[102] Dixon, Francis W. "The Home-going of a Child of God." Lansdowne Bible School and Postal Fellowship (Lansdowne Baptist Church, Bournemouth, England, August, 1963).

[103] Jernigan, John C. *Sermon Outlines With Helps, Vol. 3.* (Chattanooga: Gospel Book House, undated), 73–74; 76. Adapted.

[104] Macpherson, Ian. *Kindlings.* (Old Tappan, New Jersey: Fleming H. Revell Company, 1969), 143.

[105] Henry, 109–112.

[106] Meyer, Spurgeon, Barnes, and Others, 74.

[107] Meyer, F. B., cited in *Funeral Sermons and Outlines.* (Grand Rapids: Baker Book House, 1955), 10–11.

[108] Conwell, 60.

[109] Mirkel, Carol. http://www.goodreads.com/quotes/292120-i-d-like-the-memory-of-me-to-be-a-happy, accessed May 29, 2013.

[110] Meyer, Spurgeon, Barnes, and Others, 100.

[111] Chapman, J. B., Editor. *The Preacher's Magazine.* (Kansas City: Nazarene Publishing House (March–April 1945)), 37.

[112] Conwell, 152–153.

[113] http://growingthroughgrief.com, accessed July 31, 2013.

[114] Powell, 39.

[115] https://bible.org/illustration/another-room, accessed August 17, 2013.

[116] strengthfortoday.wordpress.com/2009/10/14/poetry-from-john-and-betty-stam, accessed August 17, 2013.

[117] Torrey, R. A. *Anecdotes and Illustrations.* (New York: Fleming H. Revell Co., 1907), Introduction.

[118] http://www.greatest-inspirational-quotes.com/death-quotes.html, accessed April 8, 2013.

[119] Rogers, Adrian. "The Day Death Died." Love Worth Finding, March 28, 2013. Oneplace.com, accessed August 8, 2013.

[120] Graham, Billy. *My Answer*—"Does God Know Everything That's Going to Happen?" Distributed by Tribune Media Services, Inc.

[121] bobrogers.me/tag/eternal-life, accessed August 20, 2013.

[122] Miller, J. R. "Afterward You Will Understand"

[123] Spurgeon, C. H. "Contentment." Sermon No. 320, delivered on Sabbath Evening, March 25th, 1860, New Park Street Chapel. www.spurgeon.org/sermons/0320.htm, accessed May 3, 2013. Bracketed comment is that of the author.

[124] "Hope After Death." sermons.logos.com/submissions/83682-Hope-after-death, accessed April 5, 2013.

[125] John R. Rice Quotes. http://christian-quotes.ochristian.com, accessed August 9, 2013.

[126] Graham, Billy, *Death and the Life After,* 43.

[127] Powell, 28.

[128] Malphurs and Willhite, 215.

[129] http://sermons.logos.com, "The Promise of Heaven." accessed July 31, 2013.

[130] Henry, 16.

Endnotes

131 Graham, Franklin and Donna Lee Toney. *Billy Graham in Quotes.* (Nashville: Thomas Nelson, 2011), 98.

132 Criswell, W. A. "In Memoriam." www.wacriswell.com, accessed April 3, 2013.

133 Shannon, Robert and J. Michael Shannon. *25 Biblical Sermon Outlines with Brisk Illustrations for Expository Preaching.* (Cincinnati: Standard Publishing, 1982), 101.

134 Ziglar, Zig. *Confessions of a Grieving Christian.* (Nashville: B and H Books, 2004), 43.

135 Spurgeon, C. H. "Precious Deaths." http://www.spurgeon.org, accessed August 19, 2013.

136 Henry, 78–79. [This statement is applicable to preaching a funeral of a suicide though directed to family and friends at large.]

137 Smith, Preserved. *The Life and Letters of Martin Luther.* (New York: Houghton Mifflin, 1911), 353–354.

138 Exell, Joseph S. *The Biblical Illustrator.* (Grand Rapids: Baker Book House, undated), 2 Samuel, 210.

139 Allen, Kerry James. *Exploring the Mind & Heart of the Prince of Preachers.* (Oswego, Illinois: Fox River Press, 2005), 106.

140 Sweeting, George. *The Joys of Successful Aging.* (Chicago: Moody Publishers, 2008), 141.

[141] Criswell, W. A. "Grief at the Death of Family/Friends." http://www.wacriswell.com, accessed April 3, 2013.

[142] Elliot, Elizabeth. http://www.goodreads.com/author/quotes/6264.Elisabeth_Elliot?page=3, accessed April 1, 2013.

[143] ibid., 42.

[144] Allen, 109.

[145] Miller, J. R. "The Beatitude of Sorrow" (1891). http://www.gracegems.org/Miller/beatitude_for_sorrow.htm, accessed March 28, 2013.

[146] thecallforward.wordpress.com, accessed April 17, 2013.

[147] Allen, 104.

[148] "Billy Graham Offers Advice on Growing Old." March 5, 2013. http://blog.christianitytoday.com/ctliveblog/archives/2013/03/billy-graham-offers-advice-on-growing-old.html, accessed April 21, 2013.

[149] Graham, Billy, *Death and the Life After,* 43.

[150] http://christian-quotes.ochristian.com, accessed April 21, 2013.

[151] Johnston and Hunter. *The Christian Treasury,* Vol. 4. (Edinburgh and London: J. R. McNair & Company, 1849), 248.

Endnotes

Morgan, 767.

Spurgeon, "Precious Deaths."

Chrysostom. *World's Greatest Sermons, Vol. 1* (Sermon "On Excessive Grief at the Death of Friends"). (New York: Funk & Wagnalls Co, 1908), 31.

Jones, G. C. *1000 Illustrations for Preaching and Teaching.* (Nashville: Broadman & Holman Publishers, 1986), 96.

Allen, 217.

Morgan, 768.

Knight, Walter. *Knights Illustrations for Today.* (Chicago: Moody Press, 1970), 95.

Spurgeon, C. H. "The Destroyer Destroyed." http://www.spurgeon.org/sermons/0166.htm, accessed July 22, 2013.

Tozer, A. W. *Rut, Rot or Revival.* (Camp Hill, Pennsylvania: Christian Publications, Inc., 1993), 140.

Saint Chrysostom. *Funeral Sermons and Outlines.* (Grand Rapids: Baker Book House, 1951), 33.

163 Hutson, Curtis, Editor. *Great Preaching on Comfort.* (Murfreesboro, Tennessee: Sword of the Lord Publishers, 1990), 164–165.

164 MacArthur, *Safe in the Arms of God*, 154.

165 Piper, John. "Funeral Meditation for Owen Glenn Shramek." www.desiringgod.org, accessed July 27, 2013.

166 Havner, Vance. *Hope Thou in God.* (Old Tappan, New Jersey: Fleming H. Revell Company, 1977), 107–108.

167 Sweeting, 141.

168 MacArthur, " Troubled Heart."

169 Cowman, C. "Consolation," p. 70. Bible.org, accessed April 6, 2013.

170 Our Daily Bread, April 17, 1995.

171 Moody, D. L. *Funeral Sermons and Outlines.* (Grand Rapids: Baker Book House, 1951), 76.

172 Henry, 75.

173 Our Daily Bread.

174 Larson, Craig Brian, Editor. *Illustrations for Preaching & Teaching.* (Grand Rapids: Baker Books, 1993), 52.

175 Powell, 50.

Endnotes

---

[176] ibid.

[177] Thomas, Gary. *Christianity Today,* October 3, 1994, 26.

[178] Source unknown.

[179] Cox, James W. Ed., *The Minister's Manual.* (New York: HarperSanFrancisco, 1995), 259.

[180] Dunn, Ronald. *When Heaven Is Silent, Trusting God When Life Hurts.* (Nashville: Thomas Nelson Publishers, 1994).

[181] Blackwood, 140.

[182] Ford, Herschel. *Simple Sermons on Heaven, Hell, and Judgment.* (Grand Rapids: Zondervan Publishing House, 1969), 23.

[183] sermonillustrations.com, accessed April 7, 2013.

[184] sermons.logos.com/submissions/102878-Illustrations, accessed March 30, 2013.

[185] Spurgeon, C. H. *Funeral Sermons and Outlines.* (Grand Rapids: Baker Book House, 1951), 12–13. [paraphrased in part]

[186] Ford, Herschel. *Simple Sermons for Funerals Services*, 30.

[187] http://www.k-state.edu/english/baker/english320/Maugham-AS.htm, accessed July 22, 2013.

188 Hobbs, H. H. *My Favorite Illustrations.* (Nashville: Broadman Press, 1990), 77.

189 ibid.

190 Morgan, 184.

191 Hutson, Curtis, Ed. *Great Preaching on Heaven.* (Murfreesboro, TN: Sword of the Lord Publishers, 1987), 15.

192 ibid.

193 Jones, G. C., 100.

194 Tan, P. L. *Encyclopedia of 7700 Illustrations: Signs of the Times.* (Garland, TX: Bible Communications, Inc., 1996).

195 ibid.

196 http://encountersministries.com/QUOTES/quotes_F.html, accessed July 22, 2013.

197 Stickney, Dorris. https://www.rainbowsbridge.com/belovedhearts/stories/doris-waterbugsanddragonflies-632617144169637500.aspx, accessed March 30, 2013

198 Tan.

199 Powell, 51.

200 Malphurs and Willhite, 238. (adapted)

[201] Henry, 66.

[202] Shelley, Bruce L. *Christian Theology in Plain Language.* (Waco, Texas: Word Books, 1985), 208.

www.ingramcontent.com/pod-product-compliance
Lightning Source LLC
Chambersburg PA
CBHW070825100426
42813CB00003B/493